# minimal

# minimal
# how to
# simplify
# your life
# and live
# sustainably

## madeleine olivia

EBURY
PRESS

10 9 8 7 6 5 4 3 2 1

Ebury Press, an imprint of Ebury Publishing
20 Vauxhall Bridge Road
London SW1V 2SA

Ebury Press is part of the Penguin Random House group of companies whose
addresses can be found at global.penguinrandomhouse.com

The information in this book has been compiled by way of general guidance in
relation to the subjects addressed. It is not a substitute and is not to be relied on
for specific professional advice. So far as the author is aware the information given
is correct and up to date as at the date of publication. The author and publishers
disclaim, as far as the law allows, any liability arising directly or indirectly from the
use, or misuse, of the information contained in this book.

First published by Ebury Press in 2020

www.penguin.co.uk

A CIP catalogue record for this book is available from the British Library

ISBN 9781529105636

Printed and bound in Great Britain by Clays Ltd, Elcograf S.p.A.

Penguin Random House is committed to a sustainable future for our business,
our readers and our planet. This book is made from Forest Stewardship Council®
certified paper.

*To my top four fans: mum Debbie, dad Mick,
sister Charlie and partner Alex. You've been there
for me through it all and always keep me afloat.*

# Contents

# Introduction

Minimal and sustainable living: a way to simplify your life, all the while doing good for our planet. Seems simple, right? Unfortunately this can be a big task, and one that many of us attempt and struggle with (me included). Lots of learning, changing and growing is involved in living more mindfully. My goal is to help you in this pursuit by sharing information and giving tips, all the while reminding you that nobody is perfect.

The way many of us currently live our lives is seriously unsustainable. We buy lots of things, throw lots away and use up lots of energy. It's how so many of us have been brought up, it's how everyone else around us does things and it's all a part of living in a convenience- and consumerist-driven world – two things which do not lend themselves to living minimally or sustainably. You have to actively go against the status quo, change learned behaviours and make an effort in your day-to-day life by saying *no*.

But going back to basics and being kinder to ourselves and the planet can be achieved with enough knowledge, experience and passion.

I have been trying out this whole 'minimalism' and 'sustainable living' for quite few years. Going vegan, decluttering, simplifying, reassessing what I buy, becoming more sustainable

and focusing on appreciating what I already have in life.
I documented a lot of this on my YouTube channel, sharing my experiences with strangers online. Which is how I got here today, writing this book.

Before this change, I was a totally different person, with a totally different focus. I grew up obsessed with fashion and beauty. While I cared about the environment, I didn't think much about how my personal habits affected the planet. I loved animals, but meat was basically my favourite food. I recycled but didn't think a great deal about single-use plastic. I was a shopaholic who dressed to impress others and wore makeup to hide my insecurities.

I had a hard time at university as I struggled with an eating disorder, social anxiety and a desperate desire to fit in. Looking back I feel sorry for past me, wishing I could explain to her that she is beautiful without makeup, and interesting without fashionable clothes. Not to mention how frustrated I feel at how much time, money and resources I wasted on items that ended up in someone else's wardrobe, down the charity shop or in the bin. I was looking for security, acceptance and attention in all the wrong places. And in doing so, I was losing the balance of what was important in life.

Towards the end of university I started to re-evaluate my life. I made big changes, such as going vegan, no longer shopping at my favourite fast-fashion outlets, skipping plastic and using my own homemade beauty products. After graduating and failing to find a job I saw a future in, I started from scratch by moving back in with my parents. This is when I started my YouTube channel.

Moving back home left me confronted by the amount of stuff I owned, and how much money I had wasted on things that meant nothing to me anymore. So I let go of a huge amount of my stuff and started to focus on what made me happy.

As I documented this decluttering process online, more and more people became interested in my honest take on minimalism, veganism and sustainable living. I found community in the people online who shared similar interests and desires to minimise and live more intentionally.

The feeling of abandoning all I knew and owned was so powerful for me. And as clichéd as it may seem, this process taught me a lot about myself and what I wanted out of life. I have learnt to take care of who I am, as well as understand my impact on this Earth. I have become more grateful, organised, thoughtful, self-aware, confident, careful, dedicated, honest and kind to myself. The knowledge and information I've gathered along the way makes me increasingly aware of the importance of spreading this message to as many people as possible. Which is why I am writing this book.

There is a stereotype of minimalists, vegans or environmentalists that make them seem like extreme activists or crazy hippies following unattainable and inaccessible lifestyles. I really want to change this impression. There are so many different versions of these 'types' (and you don't have to label yourself as any of them either). You can take elements of all or some of these lifestyles, and make them your own. You can still be a normal person while giving a shit!

I want to share the simple ways you can declutter your life, reduce waste, make your own beauty products, shop less, practise self-care, cook plants and not beat yourself up about messing up during the process. If we are to make a significant difference, we need to make this way of living more accessible to all. These changes can be as realistic and small as you want them to be. I'm not a lifestyle 'guru', I'm not perfect and I'm certainly not an expert in any of these things (except for maybe cooking a totally delicious vegan meal). I've learnt this information through my own research from other experts who are leading the way. I'm just a normal person trying to make positive changes to exist more consciously, find deeper meaning in life and reduce my footprint on this Earth. Hopefully I can inspire you to do the same.

But why is this so important?

You may have heard of a little thing called 'climate change'. Unfortunately we've got ourselves into a situation where if we don't change what we're currently doing, the future isn't looking ideal, to put it mildly. Temperatures are heating up, ice is melting, sea levels are rising, the ocean is suffering, extreme weather is occurring more frequently and animals are going extinct. Climate-change deniers need to start listening to science. These conditions aren't normal and this drastic change in our climate is being caused by humans.

We seem to have forgotten how to live at one with our Earth and instead have become lost in our own greed. Indigenous people and those living in low-income countries are on the frontlines of climate change, and they're already experiencing its effects. They are the most vulnerable, as they rely on the land and its resources for survival, yet they are contributing the least to the climate crisis and instead are trying to protect the land they live on. All the while, high-income countries continue to pump out new things for exceptionally cheap prices, use fossil fuels on a massive scale, factory farm animals and cover everything in plastic, in turn damaging our already fragile planet.

If we don't do something about this soon (and by soon we're talking in the next 12 years, or even 18 months as some experts are now saying[2]), we will reach the point of no return where nothing can be done to stop global warming and its catastrophic consequences. This is not a drill, people; we're talking species extinction.

A mass movement and overhaul of society is required to stop the worst from happening, and political action is needed. Capitalism has enabled so many of us to grow our incomes, consume more crap we don't need and use way more resources than we should be allowing ourselves. We need to stop the hustle culture, flaunting what we own and constantly striving for more more more. Instead, we need to make people strive for *less*. Less stuff, less work and less greed.

We need to minimise on a worldwide scale. Public attitudes are already changing, but are the top 1 per cent listening?

The final thing I want to say is that this is complicated. It's far more than individual change. Systematic change is needed to combat the climate crisis. On top of this, there are many parts of 'living sustainability' that aren't accessible to all. Being vegan isn't something everybody can or should do, avoiding flying or shopping from sustainable brands can be expensive – even using plastic is sometimes unavoidable. The title of the book is *Minimal* for a reason; the focus needs to be on *minimising* rather than completely cutting everything out. So take from this book what applies to *you*.

Throughout this whole learning curve, try to do this for *you* first and foremost. Care enough about yourself that you can care about the planet you live on, the people you share it with and the children that may have to deal with the mess we've made. Keep learning, push yourself to understand your connection to nature, show respect to the planet and be grateful for the life you have. Our efforts will be significant only if we empower ourselves, rather than feel shamed, into making these changes in our lives. We've all done damage, but we can all make an effort to minimise any damage we do in the future. It's a balancing act I am continuously learning, and will probably never be perfect at. But I now know the line between doing my best and pushing myself to do things that aren't good for me or my health. You should always be asking yourself where you can be better, all the while remembering to cut yourself some slack!

So who's ready to start minimising?

# one

—

# minimalism

# What is Minimalism?

'Minimalism is a tool to rid yourself of life's excess in favour of focusing on what's important – so you can find happiness, fulfilment and freedom.' – The Minimalists[1]

You may have seen the word minimalism floating around and thought, 'I could never be a minimalist, I have far too much stuff!'. This was me just a few years ago, with a wardrobe over-flowing with clothes that I never wore, a bathroom brimming with toiletries that I didn't use and a feeling that something wasn't quite right. But when I came across videos, articles and people online raving about minimalism, I became inspired to own less. I was intrigued with the idea that by decluttering, physically and mentally, you could be more conscious in your decisions and gain more fulfilment from your life.

We are so governed by *things*. In a world where capitalism reigns supreme, we're taught to aspire to a big house filled with the stuff of our dreams. Things give us instant gratification and a sense of pride. They're a physical reminder of what we have achieved. But should we be placing so much worth on our stuff? What if we flipped it on its head and instead of aspiring to owning things, we aspired to simplifying our lives and doing what makes us happy?

So much of what we see in the media is about buying and owning stuff. We're sold a dream by big brands pushing their products. We're in a vicious cycle of being convinced that if we buy a new shampoo, our hair will look better and we'll attract the perfect partner. If we own an expensive car, we'll impress our friends and feel more confident. If we own this new phone, we'll be able to take better photos to post on social media. Where does it end?

There comes a point where we have to look at what we're aspiring to, ask ourselves why, and where this idea has come from. Is it really making you happy to spend all of your money on *stuff*? Do you really need all the things you own? What would happen if you got rid of some, or a lot, of it – or if you only bought things that had a real purpose or meaning? I used to think I needed all of my different pairs of shoes, heels and dresses so that I could combine as many different outfits as possible. And yet I often looked at my clothes and felt like I had nothing to wear. The sheer volume of clothing was overwhelming to me. So I decluttered, reduced and only kept what I wore and loved.

Success is often equated to what you own, your job and how hard you work. But why can't success be about how happy you are, how good a friend you are, or how you help others? Success simply means achieving a desired aim or result, and this definition knows no boundaries. What if we chased what we really desired, rather than what we thought we should desire?

Ask yourself what you really want in life. What is necessary, and what is superfluous? Everything that doesn't make you happy, or serve a purpose, can be removed, and space can therefore be freed up to do with it what you want.

A big misconception that I want to squash is that minimalism is all about owning barely any stuff. While reducing what you own is a part of minimalism, how *much* you own is arbitrary. It is a tool to minimise the areas of your life that aren't giving you anything back, and being mindful of what you consume. By decluttering, you allow space for the things that are important. You really don't have to be a 'minimalist' in the stereotypical sense in order to use minimalism in your life. You can collect things, get enjoyment from them, and still call yourself a minimalist. You will become more aware of what you have in your life, and more conscious of the new things you bring in. But how much stuff you end up owning is individual to you.

In this journey it's therefore important not to get caught up in trying to own as little as possible. Never compare how much *you* own to anyone else. It's irrelevant. The only thing that matters is figuring out what works for you. Don't force yourself to get rid of things just because you feel you should. You don't want to impulsively get rid of something, only to buy it again somewhere down the line (I've definitely made this mistake). As you reduce, you'll start to understand what you will or won't miss. You're likely to make a few mistakes and learn from them. It can be tricky, but you'll get there.

Since decluttering, I still own quite a lot of clothes. Someone might look at my wardrobe and not imagine I called myself a 'minimalist'. There's colour, variety and lots of options. But, I've downsized to a point that works for me. I have a capsule wardrobe of clothes I love and wear. I wear the same outfits over and over. I know what I own and it makes it easy for me to get dressed every day and feel like myself. Every time I buy a new piece of clothing, I am conscious of where I am getting it from, whether I'll wear it, and if it will fit with the clothes I already own. This is a huge transformation from the person who would spend her money on anything she thought was cute.

And this is a way that I've used minimalism to fit *me*. Using what works, and leaving what doesn't. Don't fall into the trap of following 'minimalism' to the point of losing *yourself*.

The choice in all of this is yours: whether you want to go to the limit and cull everything but the basics and count how many items you own. Or whether you want to declutter and simplify to just the things you love, while still owning a variety of material things in your life.

Minimalism can be used to declutter not only material things, but to help with stress, insecurities, societal pressures and over consumption. There are so many facets that go beyond the physical, and allow you to be more grateful, conscious and happy with your life. After all, this is the whole point: to reduce to make room for what's important. The philosophy of minimalism is all about removing the distractions in order to return to the basics of what makes us happy.

So ask yourself: what are your priorities? Are the physical things in your life the most important part? Think about what makes you really happy and what you want out of life, and try to focus on the immaterial.

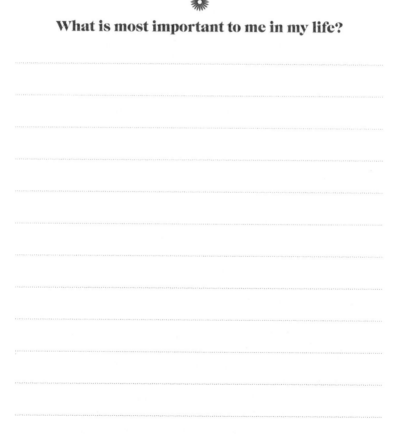

## What is most important to me in my life?

✳

# What are you doing in life that isn't helping you or having a positive impact?

SCROLLING ON MY PHONE

COMPARING MYSELF TO OTHERS

# How Minimalism Has Improved My Life and How It Can for You Too

I want to share with you some of the biggest ways minimalism has helped me and what it can do for you. It goes beyond living in a nice white apartment with only a few pieces of furniture, and stretches to how we feel, how we live and how we treat ourselves and others. For me it really has changed the decisions I make on a regular basis and my approach to life in general.

## Saving money

Letting go of my shopaholic tendencies has inevitably led to me saving a lot of money, and hopefully your bank account will benefit also. I used to live in a constant cycle of earning money to buy new things that I desperately wanted. But the problem was that I was never fully satisfied (and always broke). I've readjusted how I see and spend my money, and for the first time in my life I have therefore been able to save up for things more important than a new pair of shoes. In being smart with your purchases, you can save money for things that will last, as well as invest in your future.

## Confidence in your own skin

I used to place so much worth on my appearance, and was forever lusting after a new beauty product or clothing item to make me feel better about myself. This only perpetuated my insecurities by teaching me that the way I looked was never good enough. So I learnt to drop the expectations and started wearing less makeup, left my hair alone to do its own thing, downsized my wardrobe and stopped attaching such a huge amount of value on what I owned or how I looked. It was honestly such a huge relief to just let go. I developed a new-found confidence in myself and my body.

If you focus less on your outer appearance, it can allow more time to look inwards and gain confidence in who you are.

There is less time to worry so much about the spot on your chin or the cellulite on your thighs (both of which are very common, I'll add). Bad days are normal, but nobody should have to spend their life feeling crap about how they look, and trying to change it by buying more stuff. Simplifying can help to switch the focus and bring greater self-confidence.

## Happier mind

I am a strong believer that minimising your life can benefit your mental health. Instead of continuing an unhappy or unhealthy cycle, doing things you don't enjoy, or buying things you can't afford, you can cut these ties and create new healthy habits that bring happiness into your life. So many stresses are created by a desire for constant newness. Unhappiness caused by not having enough money for everything we're told to aspire for. Unworthiness from not having the things others seem to have so easily. An overwhelming feeling of lack. Minimalism instead gives us a feeling of abundance, of gratitude for everything we do have. It helps us to focus on what's already there, and creates a positive space for us to go after what we want, and leave behind anything that isn't making us happy anymore.

## Organisation

It's inevitable that in owning less stuff your life becomes more organised and tidy. Gone are the days of a constant 'floordrobe' and endless incomplete to-do lists. Fewer things means less mess to deal with! Yes, my home still gets messy, and yes, I regularly don't finish my to-do list, but in general my life is just that little bit less all over the place. And I ain't mad about it.

## Growth, goals and ambitions

Probably the most powerful way in which minimalism has changed my life is the fact that I have been able to focus on my self-growth and pursue my dreams. If you said to me six or seven years ago – when I was in the depths of an eating disorder, binge drinking every week, avoiding classes because of social anxiety and without a clue about what I was going to do in the future – that I would be working for myself and writing a book, I would never have believed you. So I want to encourage you to remove the distractions like I did, and chase after whatever it is you've always wanted to do. Go after it wholeheartedly and focus hard on your goals and ambitions in life, whatever they may be.

## Taking care of the planet

Minimalism has played a big part in reducing the amount of waste and resources I'm using. One of the biggest things you can do to be more environmentally friendly overall is simply to not consume as much *stuff*. Minimalism therefore facilitates a much lower carbon footprint. So if you want to change one thing to do the planet a favour, stop buying so much and start being a conscious consumer.

## Reevaluating what's truly important

Over the last few years I have let go of a lot of preconceived ideas about what I should be doing, or what other people expected me to do. Instead, I've let go of my fear and focused on what *I* want to do. I am no longer wasting an unreasonable amount of time on things that have little value; things that are only gratifying in the moment. The simplification of my life has made me discover what I want – truly, honestly and authentically. Not because of the pressures of others, or the pressures of society. The discovery of what you want isn't necessarily easy, and it can change constantly. But you've got to go for it! Getting rid of all the noise allows you to see what really matters to you.

# How to Declutter Sustainably

Before we get stuck into the decluttering, I want to share some ways you can do this responsibly and sustainably. While minimalism will no doubt lead to you becoming more eco-friendly simply because you'll be buying and using less, the process of getting rid of your things can quickly become very wasteful.

In the early days of decluttering I definitely got rid of things I could have used up, threw broken bits away I could have repurposed, or donated clothes to the charity shop that may now be in landfill. I've learnt from my mistakes, and over time have learnt to declutter more sustainably. There is no use throwing things that can be donated, re-used or recycled in the bin. Decluttering can be a long and stressful process, so I can sympathise with the temptation to just put everything in boxes and take them down to the dump. Out of sight, out of mind, right?

But there is no such thing as 'away' in this world. Humans create a lot of waste, so in our effort to be less wasteful and more minimal, we should keep this in the back of our minds. Is there a friend who might find use in this? Can I use this item for another purpose? Will a charity shop/women's shelter/homeless shelter benefit from this donation?

After being faced with all the things I had barely used or worn during the decluttering process, I've become a much more mindful shopper. Decluttering acts as a lesson to make more conscious choices in the future, so you don't repeat the past and allow things to end up being wasted.

**Here are my favourite ways to declutter sustainably:**

### FINISH IT

Small amount of shampoo left in an old bottle? Put it in the shower to use up. Too many candles? Burn them. A bag of random legumes or grains you're yet to eat? Google a recipe and add it to this week's meal plan. Find ways to use up things you want to declutter, instead of throwing them away.

### REPURPOSE

Repurposing items you want to declutter can be a really great way to use things up. Get creative and find ways to repurpose unwanted items. See pages 73–76 for my top tips for reusing and repurposing.

### SWAP WITH OR GIVE TO A FRIEND

If you don't want it, someone else might! Host a clothes swap with your friends, or just give your unworn or unused clothes, makeup, shoes, etc, to them. Not only will they be happy if they end up with something they love, but it will give your friends their shopping hit for the month.

### DECLUTTER SLOWLY

You might be on a roll and ready to fill up the car to deliver at your local charity shop, but hold fire. Try decluttering slowly and don't put too much pressure on yourself to get rid of everything right away. You have time, and time will enable you to make more sustainable choices when getting rid of your stuff.

### SELL ONLINE

A huge benefit of saying goodbye to your unwanted items is making some money! If it cost you a lot to begin with, there is a chance you can make some of that back by selling online. Technology, high-quality/designer/branded clothes and accessories, furniture and collector's items tend to sell easily. I've got into the cycle now that whenever I upgrade my camera or laptop, for example, I will sell the old one as a contribution towards the new one (which I try to buy secondhand).

## SEPARATE, THEN DONATE

Instead of piling everything up to be donated to one charity shop down the road, try separating your donations to make sure they go to a good home where they're needed. Send your unused makeup to a women's shelter; your old shoes or blankets to a homeless shelter; notebooks, folders or textbooks to a local school; old towels to an animal shelter; or books to the local library or bookshop. Think outside the box and find places where items can definitely be used.

## GIVE IT AWAY FOR FREE

One person's trash is another person's treasure! If something isn't worth enough money to sell but is still in good working order, or you need it gone straight away, pass it on for free. Freecycle is a popular choice, but there are also local Facebook groups designed for the purpose of getting rid of your unwanted stuff. Or put it outside your house with a sign saying 'free' and maybe you'll make someone's day.

## RECYCLE OR COMPOST

And if all of the above fails, make sure to recycle or compost. Cardboard, wood, glass, plastics, metals, cables, dead plants, old mattresses, fridges, broken furniture and so much more can be taken to your local recycling centre rather than the landfill. Find out more about recycling on page 77–80.

## Before you begin

Where to start? If you're a hoarder, or a shopaholic, even the thought of decluttering may seem overwhelming right now. Stuff *is* overwhelming, especially if you have a lot of it.

But it doesn't need to be complicated, and you don't need to stress yourself out over the idea that everything in your life needs to go. It doesn't. You can keep everything that you love, that makes you happy, and that has a purpose in your life. In turn, you can let go of things that you don't love, that don't make you happy, and don't have any purpose in your life.

## Understand the why

Why do you want to minimise your life? Do you want a tidier home? Do you need to get out of debt? Is it an act of self-love? Find your motivation for decluttering, to get you through this process. Maybe set a goal in your mind of what you want to achieve at the end, as well as a loose time frame of when you want to achieve this by. Specifying and setting goals in all walks of life is a good idea, as it will support you as you reach your goals.

## My decluttering goals

## Shopping ban

I know you're super excited to get stuck in, start decluttering and become a Minimalist Queen (or King). But I'm gonna have to stop you in your tracks. Before you begin this journey, it's *so* important to curb your spending habits. There's a chance that if you're feeling the urge to declutter and minimise, you may have a history of shopping just that *little bit* too much.

As soon as I found out about minimalism, one of the first things I knew I had to do was stop shopping. I acknowledged I had a problem, and quickly realised that bringing anything new into my home would only hinder the progress I wanted to make.

If you have a bit of a shopping problem, try to avoid the shops altogether (even if your friend invites you – suggest somewhere else), delete sale emails and stop consuming any media that encourages you to buy.

Well, that sounds boring, doesn't it?

Maybe to begin with, but you're likely to find that as you start to declutter, you become much more grateful for what you already own. And something even weirder may happen: you may even start to enjoy decluttering and organising your things *more* than shopping. Quit the shopping habit, and make decluttering your new hobby.

If in doubt whether you should be buying something, ask yourself these questions:

- Can I afford it?
- Do I have something similar that is good enough?
- Will I only use it once, and if so, can I borrow it from a friend instead?
- Is this an impulse buy?
- Am I buying it because of the brand name?
- Can I live without it?
- Am I buying it to impress others?
- Would I buy it if it was triple the price?
- Am I buying it out of boredom?
- Does it fit me and my style?
- Do I have clothes at home to pair it with?

It's time we stopped placing so much worth on *things*, and stopped shopping for shit we don't need. Get your head out of that bubble, ignore outside voices and only listen to your gut. Don't get caught up listening to advertising campaigns, influencers and celebrities that make you feel like you need something they're selling in order to feel better about yourself. Constantly consuming and wanting more more more can cause a big strain on our happiness. There is nothing healthy about stretching our wallets to achieve unattainable material goals. If you can change just one thing, then limiting your shopping habits – and only buying what you need and truly love – is it.

If you're struggling with saving money or have lots of debt, this is an opportunity to look at your spending habits. Everyone's situation is different, so I won't presume to understand yours, but being more intentional with what you're buying, and setting yourself a budget can work wonders over time to get yourself out of a money rut.

## What are you spending your money on regularly that you could stop, or reduce?

# Simple Tricks to Stop Shopping:

- Save it for later in a bookmark on your computer, on Pinterest or write it down.
- Avoid shops, malls and shopping centres altogether.
- Unsubscribe from your favourite shops' newsletters.
- Set yourself a monthly budget and stick to it.
- Unfollow people online who encourage you to spend money.
- Set yourself a target to save a certain amount by a certain time to give you more incentive not to spend.
- Declutter and tidy when you get the urge to buy something.
- Try renting or borrowing instead of buying something new.
- Go thrifting or secondhand shopping to get your fix without spending so much money.
- Pay with cash over card to keep track of your money better.

## Challenge!

Why not try out a no-spend challenge? Don't spend *any* money for a whole day, or only spend money on the essentials for the next week/month!

## Create a budget

Creating a budget can transform how you use and spend money. It helps you to understand where you're spending your money, and where you can improve. It can be hard to plan for the future or save money if you don't stick to a budget. We all want to avoid obsessing about money, and I used to hate even thinking about it, but facing it front on and being more mindful of my spending habits is what got me on a straight path to being more financially secure. After all, you spend all this time working hard to earn money, you ought to know where it's all going.

1 FIGURE OUT YOUR **MONTHLY INCOME**
   How much money is coming in each month? If it varies, take an average of the last three months.

2 FIGURE OUT YOUR **MONTHLY ESSENTIAL EXPENSES**
   Rent, mortgage, bills, insurance, food, drink, petrol, train tickets, household item top-ups, etc. Only stick to the basics for this part. Again, take an average of the last three months to see how much you're spending.

3 FIGURE OUT YOUR **MONTHLY NON-ESSENTIAL EXPENSES**

   Clothing, eating out, subscriptions, gym membership, daily coffee trips, taxis, takeaways, nights out drinking, beauty treatments, etc. To get a clear picture, delve into your statement and note down everything you're spending your money on outside of the essentials. Go back three months and get an average.

4 EVALUATE
   How does your income match up to your expenses? In order to save or reduce debt, you need to be earning more than you're spending. It's as simple as that. Be totally honest with yourself and evaluate where you're spending money unnecessarily within your budget. This could be eating or drinking out too

often or a monthly beauty treatment that you can't really afford. Maybe your food shop has got a bit out of hand or you're paying far too much money for your phone. Find out ways in which you can reduce your expenses significantly, particularly the non-essentials.

5   SET A **GOAL**

Do you have a goal of how much money you want to pay off, or how much money you want to save? This will be the incentive behind your budget, and will help to keep you on track. Do some maths, and set a time period for when you want to achieve this goal. Find out about how much money you need to put aside each month in order to achieve your goal.

6   CREATE YOUR **BUDGET**

Based on what you've found out, you can now put together a monthly budget to achieve your goals. Calculate how much you want to be spending each month, allowing for the essentials and non-essentials. Depending on how much you are aiming to pay or save, limit the non-essentials and prioritise the essentials to lower costs.

7   REPEAT

A few months down the line go through this process again and see how you got on. You can re-evaluate the process and set a new target and budget for your life.

✻

| INCOME | |
|---|---|
| Current monthly income | £ |

| BUDGET | |
|---|---|
| Ideal monthly budget | £ |

Essentials

**FOOD**                                    £
**TRAVEL**
**BILLS**

Non-essentials I will allow

**EATING OUT**                              £
**SOCIALISING WITH FRIENDS**
**SUBSCRIPTION TO NETFLIX**

| SAVINGS | |
|---|---|

Non-essentials I want to avoid
(amount I spend and could be saving)                    £

**NEW CLOTHES**
**TAKEAWAY COFFEE**

## Take it slow

There is no rush. You have all the time in the world to declutter, so remember to take it step by step. There is no use in becoming overwhelmed at the seemingly huge task in front of you. I remember looking at my overstuffed mess of a wardrobe, wondering how on earth I'd ever get through it. Instead of throwing in the towel and giving up altogether, I started slowly. I took everything out of my wardrobe and spent an hour or two going through it all. I didn't touch my chest of drawers, or the mountain of clothes piled on a shelf at the top of the wardrobe. I just stuck to one area of my closet and tackled it. This stopped that awful feeling you get when you start to tidy your room with bubbling enthusiasm, only to get halfway through and hate yourself for even starting.

To steer clear of ending up with a big pile of clothes in the corner of your room for a week, take it slow. Focus on one area of your home, one area of your wardrobe – one drawer even – and go from there. Over time these steps *will* add up.

## Questions to ask yourself

Here are some questions to ask yourself when going through your things to make your decisions a little bit easier. Hopefully the answers will be immediately obvious, but if you're unsure, just put it into your maybe pile to make a decision on later.

- Do I love it?
- Does it make me happy?
- Does it fit me well?
- Is it uncomfortable?
- Do I wear/use it regularly (in the last 3–6 months)?
- Is it practical?
- Is it good quality/condition?
- Do I have more than one of this item?
- Does it fit with everything else in my life, stylistically and practically?
- Is it out of date?
- Does it take up too much space?

## Try not to get carried away

During this process, you may declutter something that, later on, you wish you hadn't. I've definitely donated a few items of clothing that I ended up regretting and replacing down the line. So to help you to avoid these kinds of mistakes, remember that you should think about the picture as a whole. Yes, we want to declutter, simplify and reduce. But we shouldn't do so at the expense of day-to-day practicalities or quality of life.

### THINK AHEAD

Will I wear this next season when it gets cold again? Will I use this, if not now, but definitely at some point in the future? There might be things around the house that you don't use on a daily or weekly basis, such as a waterproof jacket or hammer, but these things are useful for you to have for when the time comes.

### DON'T COMPARE

Maybe I sound like a broken record, but: Please. Don't. Compare. Especially to bloggers online, or even to me! Nobody else's life is relevant to yours. What you own is only relevant to you, so don't feel under pressure to declutter more just to fit into a particular version of what you see minimalism to be.

### KEEP TO YOUR OWN STUFF

If you're anything like me, and live with someone who doesn't necessarily subscribe to the idea of minimalism, then leave them to deal with their own things. Declutter your own, and hopefully over time they'll join you in your endeavours for a simpler life.

### FIND A WAY TO REPURPOSE OR USE IT UP

There are many items that it's tempting to just throw away that we could definitely make the effort to use up or repurpose. Toiletries, for example, are tempting to get rid of if you have too many of them. But be practical and sustainable in your approach. If you have multiple foundations that you have built up, try to use them! Same goes for food, don't throw anything away that could be eaten. I share lots of ideas in the following sections on ways to repurpose or use particular items. Get creative and try to find a way to use them.

## Learning how to say goodbye

Some items are particularly difficult to say goodbye to. Particularly sentimental items, gifts from family and friends, or things you've spent a lot of money on. Sometimes we'll hold on to these things, even though we don't use them or like them. Here are some things to think about when faced with these more difficult items:

- Do you use this item?
- Do you actually like it, or are you keeping it because it is sentimental/a gift/expensive?
- Is there a memory or person held within this object?
- If this item were stolen or taken from you, would you be devastated? Would you replace it?
- Can you sell it and allow someone else to get value from it that you don't?
- Could you pass it on to a friend who you know would love and treasure it more than you do?
- If you don't want to get rid of it, is there a way you can use it better than it is currently being used?

Once you head into the next section and start decluttering, revisit this section when you're finding it difficult to detach. Sometimes it's hard to know where to draw the line, but we have to learn to let go when our gut is telling us to.

# How to Declutter Your Life

Looking at all you have can leave you feeling overwhelmed at where to even begin. Getting rid of things you've had for years, things that hold sentimental value and things that you've kept for that special day are often the hardest to get rid of.

## Things to get rid of now

If you want to do an initial sweep of your home, without having to make any decisions, these are some things that you can get rid of (or repurpose) today. Declutter anything that fits the descriptions below:

- Expired items
- Items you haven't worn or used in over two years
- Broken/irreparable items
- Mystery items that you don't know the purpose of
- Old and out-of-date papers, documents and receipts
- Unused kids' and pets' toys
- Incomplete items with something missing
- Stained/worn items
- Unfinished projects that you know you won't be finishing
- Duplicates that you don't need

✳

# Simple 5-step guide

So it's time for my simple 5-step guide to decluttering your life. This can be used for any of your belongings or areas of your life.

Take this at your own pace, focus on areas that are particularly cluttered, and revisit the questions on page 27 if in doubt.

## Step 1: Choose an area

OPTION 1

Start by choosing a category of things to declutter (e.g. clothing, toiletries, kitchen). You can either get stuck into the more difficult or cluttered areas, or start with something easy and less daunting. This option is great if you have a lot of stuff so it won't feel as overwhelming.

OPTION 2

Choose a physical area of your home to start with: a hanging rail, chest of drawers or storage box. This might work better if you have a lot of stuff to declutter, or really want to get stuck in by culling a lot in one go.

## Step 2: Take everything out

Things have a knack for sneakily hiding in the depths of cupboards, wardrobes and drawers. It's so much easier to clean out if you physically remove the item from where it's hiding. Whatever you've chosen to start decluttering, remove everything from where they were, and pile them on your bed, living room floor, wherever. No exceptions.

## Step 3: Make piles

Now it's time to get stuck in and start making decisions. We're going to make three piles: yes, no and maybe.

### YES

Things you use regularly (every week for example) and/or absolutely love. This can also include things you love, but maybe need fixing or repairing – just be sure that you *will* actually fix or repair them. They're practical, make you feel good, and should be a no-brainer in this decision making.

### NO

Things you haven't used in the last six months to a year, and no longer love. They don't fit, they aren't practical, you already have two other versions of the same thing or they just don't make you feel good. This can also include items that you intended to fix or update, but know you'll never get around to. It's time to go.

### MAYBE

Things you don't use very often and you're not sure if you love or not. Maybe they don't fit too well, but they're a gorgeous colour. Or maybe it's a cool gadget that you just never get around to using. This can also include items you want to fix but are unsure you will have the time or money to. If you're even slightly unsure about an item, put it in this pile.

## Step 4: Sort

Everything you said yes to can be put back where it belongs.
This can give you an opportunity to do a bit of re-organising and
neatening up. Colour-coordinate your wardrobe, fold things neatly,
put dividers in your drawers, store things away in mason jars or
containers, and make sense of all of the stuff you're keeping. Find a
home for everything. This process can be one of the most satisfying
parts of minimising your space.

If you're keeping something and repurposing/fixing it, put this
somewhere separately for you to be reminded to complete this
project. It's a great idea to set a time limit on this so that if you
don't get around to fixing it, it goes. This is a good incentive to
make you get it done.

NO = SEPARATE

Separate into piles: donating, selling, recycling or throwing away.

MAYBE = REVISIT

Go through the maybes with a fine toothcomb. Do you really love
them? Do you use it often? Does it fit you well? Look over the
questions from page 27 and be totally honest with yourself, while
also remembering not to force yourself to get rid of anything you
may end up replacing or regretting further down the line. If the
answer is no to any of the questions, you've guessed it, they're going
back in that no pile to be sorted.

## Step 5: Get rid

You'll want to root through the things you've said **no** to and decide what items you're going to be selling, donating or recycling.

### SELL

Any items that are designer/good-quality/trendy you can try selling. Some of my favourite places to sell clothes are on Depop or eBay, and a great place to sell furniture is Facebook Marketplace or Gumtree. Nowadays there are so many apps and websites out there to sell your unwanted items.

A word of caution, however: don't let the sell pile become bigger than the donate pile. Know how much effort and time you're willing to put into selling your things, whether they're going to end up sitting in your hallway for the next month, and if you think they'll make much money. You know yourself best, so be honest and make a considered decision. Try reducing the price if they're not budging, or add them to your donate pile if your sale isn't successful.

### DONATE/GIFT

Everything that is in good condition but you don't want to sell can be donated. This is the feelgood part! I love taking my unwanted clothes around to my friends' houses for them to try! But probably the easiest option is to simply donate to a local charity/thrift shop. You can also find out to see if there are any other places locally that take donations, such as homeless charities, schools, animal shelters, vintage shops and reclamation yards. Try to be mindful of the best place to donate your unwanted items.

### RECYCLE

Finally, if there are items that are heavily stained, ripped or beyond repair, it's time for them to be recycled. Gross old curtains? Recycle them. Half-empty moisturiser you're never going to finish? Clean and recycle it. Visit or call up your local recycling centre to find out what they do and don't recycle.

# Notes

# ① CHOOSE AN AREA

## CATEGORY

CLOTHING
TOILETRIES
KITCHEN

## AREA

HANGING RAIL
CHEST OF DRAWERS
STORAGE BOXES

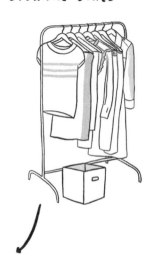

# ② TAKE EVERYTHING OUT

# Clothing, Toiletries and Beauty

## Clothing

It's pretty easy to find clothes in your wardrobe that have been left untouched for years, or maybe never even worn. Sort through, pass them on to a friend or donate today. Our bodies change over time, clothes get old, and there's no use wearing something too small, uncomfortable, or that doesn't make you feel your best.

## Shoes

It's easy to collect shoes that you aren't wearing day-to-day. If a pair are worth money, try selling them online. Or maybe you have a friend you know would put them to good use. Donation is also a great option and many charities will accept used shoes.

## Toiletries and makeup

Skin lotions and potions you were told would solve your skin issues (but haven't) need to go. This also goes for any makeup brushes: only keep the ones you use! Old ones can be a great cleaning tool, or used as children's paintbrushes. Donate any unopened and in-date toiletries and makeup to your local women's shelter, or offer to your friends. If anything is out of date or opened, wash and recycle the plastic packaging.

## Handbags

I used to be quite the collector of handbags, until I realised I was only using a small handful of them. So even if it's really pretty, if you aren't wearing it, it's time to get rid. If it cost you a lot of money, try selling on Depop, eBay or Vestaire Collective.

## Jewellery

As we grow older our style may change. Minimise to only the jewellery that you love wearing, or that holds sentimental value.

# Kitchen

### Fridge and food pantry

Sell-by dates can't always be trusted, so give the food in your kitchen a good sniff and compost what isn't fresh (recycle the packaging if you can). This can be a good reminder to meal plan in the future and stick to your list when grocery shopping, so less food goes to waste. Put anything that is nearing its shelf life on your meal plan for the week.

### Tupperware

I think my mum passed on the desire to re-use and collect old plastic containers (remember the days when your school lunch was packed in an old ice-cream container?). While this is a great way of repurposing, if you have too many filling up your cupboard that you don't use, and ones that are far too old to be storing food anymore, it's time to recycle or repurpose them (they can make great drawer dividers).

### Crockery and utensils

If you've upgraded to a new blender, then give away your old one. If you've ended up with two cheese graters or a few ice trays, donate the ones you don't use. Ask around, and you might be surprised who needs something! Plus you'll free up space by only keeping what you need and use in your kitchen.

### Equipment and appliances

You bought your juicer with good intentions, but the morning juices just haven't become a reality. That ice-cream maker you got as a gift has never seen ice cream in its life. So if you have a kitchen appliance that's sitting at the back of a kitchen cupboard gathering dust, donate it to the charity shop, sell it or find some-one you know would love it!

# Miscellaneous

### Books/magazines

We all love our books. But if it's been sitting on your shelf and you know you won't be reading it, pass it along. If you've read it and won't be reading it again, then it's time to donate! Library cards and Kindles can be a wonderful alternative to buying a physical book if you already have too many.

### Documents/papers

Shred those old bank statements and bills. If you're worried about any information you may need in the future, take a photo and save in a file on your computer just in case.

### Notepads and stationery

Get all the pens you own together and start scribbling. If it doesn't work, it's time to go. In the future, stick to buying pens you know you like writing with, or opt for a fountain pen that you can top up. Recycle notepads that are totally full. If they have a few empty pages left, pop them on your desk at work to use for quick notes.

### Electronics, gadgets and wires

Whether it's an old iPod or a second camera – if you don't use it then sell it on eBay for some extra cash. Some companies will also let you send your phone back in exchange for money. I don't know about you, but wires end up infiltrating every corner of my home. Go through and recycle any that came with old gadgets.

### DVDs, CDs and games/toys

By all means keep your favourite DVDs or CDs, but try signing up to some streaming services to free up some physical space in your home. And if you aren't playing the games in your cupboard, then maybe a child at a local children's hospital will!

# Home Decor, Furniture and Sentimental

### Trinkets, gifts and seasonal items

Gifts can be really tricky to get rid of. A loved one took time to buy something for you out of the kindness of their hearts. Just remember that the thought is still there, and the kindness has been given. If you aren't using it or you don't like it, find someone who *will* use it or *will* like it. If you've kept birthday cards, sort out which ones are meaningful.

### Linen/towels

Old and stained beach towels and bed linen you never use are better off used as rags for DIY, donated to an animal shelter or put in the recycling bin. Keep it simple and stick to what you need and love.

### Furniture and decor

Get rid of anything that you no longer enjoy, or that doesn't have a purpose. It's pretty easy these days to sell your furniture, or even give it away for free. If it just needs some fixing up, try an upcycling project. A lick of paint and a new set of handles can transform a piece of furniture. Getting rid of decorative trinkets around the home can be one of the best ways to make your home feel less cluttered.

### Sentimental items

Sentimental items are some of the hardest to declutter. Don't overwhelm yourself with this and be sure of any decisions you make. I left lots of my sentimental items until the end so I had got into the swing of things first. Go through and only keep what truly brings back happy memories and you feel you need in your life. Sometimes saying goodbye is hard, but necessary. Listen to your gut. Keep a pretty memory box for everything important to you.

# Digital Workspace and Other

### Social media

Social media can be a dangerous place. Unfollow anyone that doesn't make you feel good about yourself, or makes you compare yourself. Even if that is a friend of yours, you can choose to 'mute' or 'hide' them from your newsfeed without causing any offence. It's your feed, and it doesn't need to be cluttered with anything but what makes you inspired and motivated, or puts a smile on your face.

### Files

Find a system to file your documents, photos and movies on your computer and hard drive and delete anything you don't need. Empty your download folder, trash and desktop periodically. Try organising and backing things up to the cloud and staying on top of everything so it doesn't get into a mess again.

### Phone

Remove any apps that you aren't using, or that you find have a negative impact on your life. This could be a social media app you're spending too much time on, or a game that you are addicted to. If it's wasting your time, or not being used, delete it. Also remember to back everything up regularly, so you can sort through photos and videos to free up space on your phone. Switch off notifications so you aren't constantly distracted.

### Emails

Go through your inbox and unsubscribe from anything that tempts you to buy stuff, that you don't read, or that you never signed up to in the first place. Organise your emails into folders and go through and delete any that you don't need. It can be hard to keep an empty inbox when your job requires lots of emailing, but try to keep the emails sitting in your inbox to a minimum.

## Workspace

A cluttered workspace can make for a cluttered mind. If you find your desk getting covered in things every time you work at it, consider getting a chest of drawers to organise all of your things. Declutter any excess stuff that isn't needed for work or doesn't make you feel motivated.

## Junk drawers

Say goodbye to the junk drawer. You don't need it in your life! Delve in and sort. All of your things deserve their own home.

# Self and Life

While this part doesn't require yes, no and maybe piles, your life also needs some decluttering. There is so much more to minimalism than just stuff!

## Relationships

There is no time in your life for people who don't support, care for and love you. If you're in a relationship (romantic or platonic) that is no longer a mutually supportive and loving one, then it's time to move on. Be strong and show yourself the self-love you deserve by not keeping people in your life who don't make you happy.

## Time

Your time is important. We live in a busy modern world where everything is go go go. Fill up your calendar. Wake up early. Go to bed late. Work work work. But your time is so valuable. Say no to events, activities, workshops and commitments that you don't want to do. You don't *have* to do them. You know what is and isn't a top priority, so don't forget that. Find time in your day or week that you can free up and make time for yourself.

## Spending habits

We've talked about this, but re-evaluating your spending habits is vital to this journey. After you've gone on your shopping ban, continue to reassess your budget and spending habits to see where your weaknesses lie, and where you can improve.

## Negative thoughts

Everyone has them. They're there to test us and to push our limits. But don't let these negative thoughts creep in and take over your life. Either ignore them, say them out loud to a friend, or write them down and process them. I find getting them out of my head helps me to rationalise what I am thinking and hear just how silly some of these negative thoughts actually are. Don't keep them cooped up in your head to fester and grow. Understand that these thoughts don't define or control you.

## Unhealthy habits

What unhealthy habits are you continuing that need to end? Are you smoking when you know it's bad for you? Dating someone who treats you like crap? Going to bed late because you're scrolling on your phone? Find ways to replace these unhealthy habits with new ones. Empower yourself to move forward with a healthier and happier attitude. Decluttering an unhealthy habit can completely transform your life.

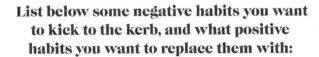

# List below some negative habits you want to kick to the kerb, and what positive habits you want to replace them with:

NEGATIVE

SCROLLING ON MY PHONE AT NIGHT

POSITIVE

PHONE OUT OF THE BEDROOM, REPLACED WITH A BOOK INSTEAD

# My Top Minimalism Hacks and Tips

I've done a lot of decluttering over the years, and along the way I've learnt a few tips and tricks to make the process a little bit easier.

1 BOXING

Taking up boxing at the weekend is the perfect way to destress from all the mess you've created. Only joking. Boxing up your things in an actual box, however, is a great trick for those of you that struggle to let go of your possessions.

Start by creating piles of **yes, no** and **maybe**. Now put everything in your **maybe** pile into a box. The trick is to put this box away in storage for a chosen period of time, say a month, and see whether you reach for anything in that box during that time period. If the month is up, and you've not reached for anything in the box, then those **maybes** can now become **nos**. I've done this quite a few times now and nine times out of ten I never reach for anything in my maybe boxes, so off to the charity shop they went!

If you're feeling brave, another box trick is to get the biggest box you can find, and just fill it up! Again, set yourself a time period – a day, a week, a month – and you have to fill the box up with things before that time is up. This can be a great way to encourage you to get serious about some items you've been holding on to.

2 HANG IT UP

If you're ready to truly find out what you wear, simply turn all your hangers in your wardrobe the wrong way around. When you wear an item of clothing, put it back the right way around. Again, set yourself a period of time (maybe this could be a longer period if you have certain items that you know you only wear for special occasions, or in specific weather) and find out which hangers remain unturned. *Et voilà!* Your deepest darkest wardrobe secrets have been revealed, and it's time to say goodbye to those unturned items.

3   DUPLICATES, DUPLICATES, DUPLICATES

We've all collected multiples of an item, maybe unintentionally.
An easy way to declutter is to reduce these duplicates. Go
through all your drawers, cupboards and closets, and find
anything that you have unnecessary spares of. I'm talking
ten different kitchen towels, five pairs of headphones, twelve
different shades of red lipstick. Pick your favourites and find
new homes for the rest.

4   ONE IN, ONE OUT

This isn't a hard and fast rule, but the 'one in, one out' rule
is something you can do as you make it further into your
decluttering experience. Every time you buy a new item,
something has to go. Not only does it make you more
considerate when you're purchasing something new, but it
means your home won't collect any new clutter. This can be a
direct replacement – you buy a new pair of jeans, you donate
an old pair – or it can be anything around your house that you
know ought to go.

5   CLEAR SURFACES

Keeping the surfaces around your home clear from clutter
will immediately leave it feeling tidier, more spacious and less
cluttered. Maybe you have a lot of kitchen equipment sitting
on your counters that you rarely use. Or your desk is covered
in stationery, paper and clutter that could be organised into
drawers. Clearing and organising these surfaces, even of excess
trinkets and home decor, will make a huge difference to the
overall feel of your home.

6   FIND TIME

Minimalism goes beyond physical stuff. We can apply it to
how we spend our time. We've all wasted one too many hours
binging an addictive TV show on Netflix, scrolled for far too
long on our phones, or scheduled things into our day that we
just don't want to be doing. Try to reclaim this time by swapping
some of these time-wasting habits for something more useful.

**Scrolling your phone at night?** Leave the phone out of the bedroom and take a book to bed with you instead.

**Waking up late every day and rushing to work?** Set your alarm and get into the routine of waking up a bit earlier and having some time for yourself. Try enjoying a slow breakfast, doing some yoga or going for a walk.

**Feeling like your whole week is booked out and there is no time to just relax?** Schedule in a day each week with no plans at all, every week. Use this time however you feel on the day, and just do whatever the hell you fancy!

Stop wasting your life away on things that don't matter to you, and instead cherish that time doing things that bring you long-term happiness.

### 7  DECLUTTER AND ORGANISE

Don't just declutter your wardrobe and throw everything back into your cupboard in a mess. Choose a system and organise everything back in neatly so it makes you feel happy when you look in that space again. If you're doing your wardrobe, for example, colour coordinate, or organise into categories. This will make keeping track of your things a lot easier in the future.

### 8  WAIT BEFORE YOU BUY

Before you go to order something online, or pick something up in the shops, give it time. Pin that pair of shoes to your wishlist, or leave the shop and go back next week if you really want to. Give yourself time to think about a purchase and discover whether it's an impulse one, or something you genuinely needed.

# Things I've Stopped Buying

If you've not done it already then now that you've decluttered, it's a good time to reevaluate your spending habits. A huge part of minimalism is what you're buying and bringing into your life. I noticed massive changes in the things I was buying as soon as I started to declutter and was faced with the amount of useless stuff I had bought over the years, and the waste I'd created as a result. I started to think of areas in which I could save money by not buying something anymore, making it myself, or finding a sustainable alternative.

There are so many things in our lives that we're conditioned to believe we need. Fancy skincare products, kitchen gadgets and upgraded technology every few months. While these things are exciting and I get enjoyment from many of them still, sometimes it's helpful to take a step outside of the bubble and notice why you're buying them. Do you really need it? Will it be useful in your life on a daily or weekly basis? Can you afford it? Do you already have something similar that does the job fine? Asking yourself questions before you make purchases can be a game changer when trying to be a conscious consumer.

Have a look through the list over the next few pages and see if there are any things you could also reduce, stop buying altogether, make yourself or find more sustainable alternatives to.

| BEAUTY PRODUCTS | SWAP |
| --- | --- |
| Hair masks/leave-in conditioners/serums | Argan/coconut/extra virgin olive oil |
| Hairspray | Homemade sea salt spray (see page 132) |
| Disposable makeup remover wipes/cotton pads | Flannel/muslin cloth/ reusable cotton pads |
| Plastic q-tips/cotton buds | Bamboo q-tips/cotton buds |
| Experimental makeup/makeup you don't use on a daily basis | Natural and multipurpose makeup that you use daily |
| Expensive or unnecessary face scrubs, toners, serums and creams | Homemade and multipurpose products that you use daily |
| Dry shampoo | Cornflour or cocoa powder |
| Heavy foundation/skin makeup | BB/CC cream or lightweight foundations |
| Packaged shower gel or body wash | Unpackaged multipurpose soap |
| Shaving foam | Coconut oil or aloe vera |
| Plastic toothbrush | Bamboo toothbrush or electric toothbrush with detachable heads |
| Dental floss | Biodegradable dental floss |
| Disposable plastic razors | Metal or safety razor |

**Stop using altogether:** Mouthwash

| HOUSEHOLD ITEMS | SWAP |
|---|---|
| Kitchen paper towels | Reusable cloths |
| Specific cleaners (window cleaner, kitchen cleaner, etc.) | Homemade and multi-purpose cleaners (recipes on pages 238–243) |
| Plastic bags | Reusable bags |
| Home trinkets and decor | Plants |
| Fabric softener | Essential oils or white vinegar |
| Air freshener | Homemade air freshener (recipe on page 240) |
| Disposable cloths and sponges | Reusable cloths and sponges |

| CLOTHES AND ACCESSORIES | SWAP |
|---|---|
| Fast fashion and trends | Secondhand and slow fashion |
| Single-wear items that aren't easily paired with existing wardrobe | Multi-wear items that work easily with existing wardrobe |
| Impractical clothes | Comfy and practical clothes |
| Costume jewellery | Minimal jewellery you wear regularly |
| Impractical handbags | Backpack or practical handbags |
| Impractical shoes | Basic and comfortable pairs that match your existing wardrobe |

**Stop using altogether:** On-sale clothes you don't actually need

| TECH | SWAP |
| --- | --- |
| CDs/DVDs | Streaming platforms |
| Poor-quality tech | Durable/longwear tech |
| Batteries | Rechargeable batteries |

**Stop using altogether:** New/trendy tech, gimmicky tech, pricey apps and subscriptions

| FOOD AND DRINK | SWAP |
| --- | --- |
| Animal products | Vegan alternatives |
| Bottled water | Reusable water bottle and water filter |
| Excessive alcohol | Alcohol in moderation |
| Pre-prepared food | Cook from scratch |

**Stop using altogether:** Multi-buy savings on food you don't usually buy, takeaway drinks, takeaway food

| MISCELLANEOUS | SWAP |
| --- | --- |
| Tampons/pads | Menstrual cup/reusable pads/ period underwear |
| Books | Library card/Kindle |
| Magazines | Online subscription |

**Stop using altogether:** Duplicates, souvenirs, multiple phone cases, branded items, sales and coupons

That was easy wasn't it? Just kidding, I know that decluttering and letting go can be hard. In fact, this whole process is something you'll keep working at every day. I still am! But once the wheels have started to turn, and you begin to see the benefits, it'll get a lot easier. After you've decluttered your stuff, you'll enjoy the extra space, the tidier rooms and the feeling of knowing what you own. You can focus more on what you want out of life, and start working on your own happiness with fewer distractions.

Hopefully one of the biggest lessons you'll have learnt from reducing is being more mindful of what you buy from now on. Putting perspective, thought and a conscious mindset behind any purchases means that you won't build up your collection of stuff again. This part is tricky too, but over time you'll get the hang of it and it'll become like second nature. You want to get to a point where you're no longer chasing things, and are content in what you have. And anything you do buy is relevant, necessary and easy. It doesn't rule your decisions, nor does it put you under any stress. If you're doing OK now with what you currently have, then you can live without it for a little bit longer.

# two

—

# waste and sustainability

# Why Reducing Waste is Important

Overconsumption, and the inevitable waste that comes with it, is one of today's most pressing issues. With plastic everywhere we look, more food being thrown away than ever before, landfills overflowing with non-recyclable plastic and our climate noticeably changing, it's time for us to make a change. More and more pressure is being put on governments worldwide to do something about the situation.

Discussion about waste and plastic usage is spreading too. Over the last few years I've seen a massive change in attitude and conversation about waste across mainstream media and in everyday conversations. Big companies are switching from plastic straws to paper straws, and are rewarding customers with reduced prices for bringing their own coffee cups. But is this currently enough?

Sadly the waste we are producing is on a scale that we've lost control of. In 2016, 5 tonnes of waste was generated per EU inhabitant[3], while in the UK we generated 222.9 million tonnes of total waste in 2016.[4] This is inevitably leading to serious issues not only for the ecosystems and animals we share this planet with, but for us as humans. Millions of tonnes of waste each year, that could otherwise decompose, is ending up in landfill and producing methane, a potent greenhouse gas.

Worldwide waste isn't equally spread across the world. Unsurprisingly, the more money a country has and the higher its rate of urbanisation, the more waste it produces. As a UK resident, my country is one of the bigger culprits. The higher our disposable income and the better our living standards, the more likely we are to consume things and services that therefore produce high amounts of waste. On top of that, those living in urban areas produce about twice the amount of waste as those living in rural areas.[5]

So much of this waste is inappropriately managed, ending up in our oceans, in landfill or being incinerated, thus contaminating the soil we walk on and the air we breathe. Two billion people on Earth are living without any waste collection, and three billion more have no controlled waste disposal, making it even harder to deal with. This poor waste management is a global crisis that is polluting rivers, the ocean and the air, while damaging human health and the economies of the countries impacted the most.[6] It is estimated that by 2050 there will be more plastic in the oceans than fish.[7]

We throw things in the bin and don't think about them again. But that item, particularly if it's plastic, will likely outlast all of us. Sadly, lots of this waste is ending up in other countries, becoming the burden of marginalised groups. High-income nations are shipping their waste to lower-income nations to deal with, not only contaminating their environment, but posing a health risk to local populations. Why is our own overconsumption someone else's problem? You wouldn't dump your trash in your neighbour's backyard, so why are we doing it to other countries?

With a growing population, there seems to be no end in sight to the plastic and waste crisis. The more people that populate this planet, the more waste we'll produce as a collective. So what's the solution? We must create less waste, and that means completely restructuring how we manage waste, and moving away from a linear economy towards a circular one. But how does any of this happen?

# What Can Be Done?

Unfortunately, I don't have all the answers. Something needs to be done on a large scale by governments and companies to lower plastic consumption and create less waste in the production line. But as an individual, I try my hardest to reduce my waste when and where I can. What I can help you with is how to individually reduce your waste and how to vote with your wallet. If we all do our bit we can collectively make a big difference. If we all say no to extra packaging, plastic and waste; buy from brands that are sustainable and ethical; and speak up about this issue, we can get those in charge to start listening. Supply and demand starts with the consumer, so we *can* influence how the producer acts and what they create by supporting the right things.

## A journey towards sustainability

I am thankful that, from a young age, my family instilled in me values that no doubt have been a big part of why I am so passionate about the environment today. They dressed me in (sometimes questionable) secondhand clothes, sewed them up when they tore, took large boxes for our shopping to the supermarket, despite the strange looks, and were recycling when nobody else around us was.

As well as being better for the environment, so many of these habits for my family, and many others, were to save costs during financially hard times. During the Second World War, 'Make Do and Mend' was encouraged as a way to cope with rationing, advising people how to be more frugal and save money. Today, however, everything is so cheap that we are much more careless. If something is broken, instead of fixing it, we buy a new one. If something goes out of fashion, we move on to the next trend. The convenience and ease of modern life perpetuates this linear economy. Why bother fixing it when we can get a brand spanking new version delivered to our door the next morning, 'on sale for 25 per cent off'?

We are influenced our whole lives by companies to buy so much stuff that we just don't need, that very often ends up in the bin. We want, we buy, we use, we throw away. Beyond the things that genuinely make us happy or serve a purpose in our life, what are we using and buying that ends up being wasteful? What areas of our life can we re-evaluate to reduce our personal waste?

In my early twenties I started to ask myself these questions, and learn more about what areas in my life I could improve in order to minimise my waste. It was an empowering journey of being more aware of myself and the consequences of my actions. I grew up with privilege: being born in a safe country, with white skin, into a middle-income family, with no health issues and the opportunity to receive a full education and therefore a well-paid job, so I can't speak from a position of experiencing the effects of the current waste or climate crisis. This is why I became so passionate about changing my actions: because I can and because I knew I should.

Aside from skipping on the plastic bottles and composting my food, my biggest change was consumption. If you want to lower your waste, it's as simple as reducing what you consume. If you're living in a higher-income country, such as the UK or the US, then by default you're producing more waste. If this is you, then you need to be more mindful of your consumption. Say no to new things, change your habits and think twice before impulse buying that cute dress you saw someone wearing on Instagram.

But, boy, has changing my habits been a journey. And I mess up all the time! And while I try my best, I am certainly not the perfect image of 'sustainability'. Mental health, physical health, work, family, relationships, money, habits and everything else in life means we should never push ourselves beyond our own limits of what it means for us to be 'sustainable'. Individual circumstances mean we can't always choose the more eco option (which in a lot of instances is a privilege that only a few have access to). Despite our best efforts, sometimes we just have to accept that we can't do it all, and we are fighting against a system that is built unsustainably.

I always try my best, and I want to encourage you to as well, but instead of beating yourself up about the mistakes you make or circumstances that are beyond your control, try to focus on the positive changes you've made. We can't expect that everyone does everything. But we can expect that everyone does *something*. The world's problems are not the responsibility of us as individuals, but us as a collective – and in particular, the individuals, companies and countries who are having the *biggest* impact.

One of the biggest lessons on my sustainability journey is that there is no such thing as being totally 'sustainable'. You may notice that I never use the phrase 'zero waste', simply because this idea is impossible. I've never referred to myself as zero waste, nor do I believe anyone can be. We all create waste; we all do things that aren't good for the environment; we all have lives that are supported by wasteful and harmful industries. We're human! Attempting to live with zero waste is a privilege very few people are able to achieve. But this doesn't mean we should throw in the towel and do nothing, it means we should just lower our waste, and do our best at it.

# How Reducing Your Waste Can Save You Money

To give you some inspiration to get you started, I thought I'd begin with some ways by which being less wasteful can save you some money. After all, being thrifty and frugal goes hand in hand with being more sustainable!

1   TURN IT OFF

    Get into the habit of switching things off when you're finished with them to save on your electricity and heating bill. It's the oldest trick in the book and one my dad has been nagging me about since I was a little girl. Switch off the lights when you leave the room, turn your TV off at the plug rather than leaving it on standby, unplug your phone when it's fully charged so you're not wasting energy. Over time, these little things will add up in energy and money saved.

2   GIVE UP BOTTLED WATER

    Getting your own reusable water bottle is one of the easiest ways to reduce your waste, while also saving money. Marketing has lead us to believe that bottled water is healthier, when the reality is that in the UK it's no safer than tap water over and 35 million plastic bottles are used every day – 23 million of these won't get recycled, which means they'll end up in landfill or in the environment[8].

3   COLD WASH

    In the shower, and with your laundry, switch to cold water. Lots of laundry detergents advise a colder wash for your clothes (it also protects your clothes better), and having a cold shower (or at least switching it to cold towards the end of your shower) can heavily save on bills and energy.

4   AIR–DRY

    Instead of tumble drying your clothes or using a hairdryer on your hair, try air–drying. Anything that creates heat requires a lot of energy, and therefore can cost a lot of money.

5 CYCLING

Get yourself a bike (buy secondhand to save some cash) and try cycling to places you would usually drive. It's a great workout, lots of fun and can make a significant difference to your carbon footprint. Plus, once you've bought the bike, it's free!

6 MAKE YOUR OWN

This can be your own hair products, clothing, artwork, gifts, cards – anything that you can get creatively involved in and make yourself. Later I will go into more detail about how to make your own cleaning and beauty products that'll save you lots of money in the long run, while avoiding toxic and harmful chemicals found in many commercial products.

7 COOK FROM SCRATCH

I'm a huge advocate for cooking and I think it's one of the most valuable tools in life. Not only will it save you a lot of money on takeaways, ready-meals and restaurant food, but it will inevitably save on plastic packaging and food waste. Head to Chapter 5 for lots of cooking tips and recipes.

8 FIX IT

Instead of throwing it out and replacing with a new one, see if you can fix it first. Learning to sew and how to do your own DIY can be a great money saver in the long run, while lengthening the life of things you own.

9 SWITCH TO RENEWABLE ENERGY

Most people stay on the same energy plan for years. Look into how much it is costing you compared to a renewable energy company. In my experience it is the same, or even cheaper. Supporting renewable energy over fossil fuels is one of the most important ways you can be more sustainable.

10 AVOID BUYING NEW

Whether it's secondhand, vintage, reclaimed, repurposed, borrowed, a hand-me-down or you found it on the side of the street, do what you can before buying something new. You'd be surprised what you can find out there.

※

## How can you reduce your waste?

List a few things that you can easily implement today. Add in any necessary details such as how you can do it, or when you want to do it by:

FIX MY JEANS RATHER THAN BUYING A NEW PAIR — USE MY MUM'S
SEWING MACHINE AND ASK HER IF SHE CAN HELP — THIS WEEKEND

# Fun and Easy Things to do to Reduce Waste

BEACH CLEAN

Bring a bag; bring a friend, or two. Visit a beach and pick up all the litter you find. Make it a regular thing! This can be done anywhere. If you live near a park, do a park clean.

COLLECT

Keep all the waste you create in one day, one week, or even one month. See the physical amount of waste you produce, and realise what areas you can improve on.

GIVE IT UP

Think of one item you buy for convenience, on a daily or weekly basis, that you can cut out altogether. Give up the convenience for the sake of the planet and think of a waste-free alternative.

BE PREPARED

Remember a fork, reusable bag and water bottle when you go out, to avoid using any extra plastic.

LOOK

Take a peek in your cupboards right now and analyse your waste; see what areas can be improved upon and take note.

VISIT

Find out if any local shops have refill stations; visit a vintage market, greengrocer, farmers' market or small businesses. Find out what you can get locally that saves on waste.

START A PETITION

What waste problem bothers you? Plastic straws? Water bottles? Fast fashion? Food waste? Write up a petition and share it online, get your friends to sign it and put in place a call to action to make a change.

# Refuse, Reduce, Reuse, Repurpose, Recycle

The 5 Rs of sustainability – refusing, reducing, reusing, repurposing and recycling – have been around for a while. Lots of people also add 'borrow' onto the end of the list as well. These Rs are the cornerstone of trying to reduce your waste and environmental impact. It serves as a reminder to everything you do. Can I refuse? Can I reduce? Can I reuse? Can I repurpose? Can I recycle?

# Refuse

At the top of our sustainability pyramid is refuse. In the previous chapter we discussed the power of saying no and buying less, and how it will make the biggest difference to your overall impact. Refusing is therefore integral to minimal living.

## Don't buy it

Whenever you go to buy something, try to think of the journey it took to get to you. It's easy to forget about this in our modern world, where at the click of a button we can get what we want within 24 hours. But the materials used in the item had to be grown, the product had to be designed by somebody, built by someone else, packaged up in plastic, shipped and transported to the country it's being sold in. The journey of any product doesn't go without waste, lots of energy and resources. By considering these things you can evaluate if the resources and excess waste are needed. Are you buying something because you need it, or because you feel like it?

## Avoid plastic-wrapped food

So much of the food in the supermarket today is wrapped in layers of unnecessary plastic. Nature was kind enough to provide fruits and vegetables with skins for their protection, so why the extra plastic? Most of this plastic isn't easily recyclable, meaning it goes straight to landfill. Sadly, lots of the food wrapped in plastic is cheaper and more convenient, making it easy for consumers to opt for the plastic-wrapped option over the unpackaged alternative. On your next food shop, opt for the plastic-free option where possible. Seek out places such as farmers' markets or greengrocers that have less plastic wrapping and commit to avoiding plastic-wrapped food when the option is available to you. Send a message by unwrapping it in the shop and leaving all the plastic at the till. Avoiding plastic often isn't easy, but weigh up your options and remain conscious of the plastic that's going into your basket.

## Bring your own bag

Plastic bags need to be a thing of the past, and this can happen if we bring our own reusable option. You don't need to go out and buy something fancy or new either. Most of us probably have some reusable bags in our home that we can use, such as a backpack or an old plastic bag. But it can sometimes be worth getting yourself a cotton tote bag or bag for life to reuse on a regular basis. If you forget your bag, don't be embarrassed to say no to a plastic bag and carry your items out with you. If you have too much stuff to carry out, ask if they have any cardboard food boxes you can use instead.

## Single-use plastic and plastic packaging

In the UK, plastic packaging accounts for 44 per cent of total plastic, but it accounts for a total of 67 per cent of *plastic* waste. Say no to plastic straws, plastic bottles, plastic cutlery, coffee cups, plastic-wrapped food and plastic bags. Bring your own reusable options and ask cafes or restaurants to put your food or drink in your own container or bag. Switch single-use for reusables when and where you can. If we want to normalise this, we have to all start saying no to single-use plastic items and unnecessary plastic packaging.

## Say no to freebies

Buy one get one free, free gifts, free pens or stickers. Say no to them if you think they'll end up in the bin pretty soon after the excitement of the freebie has worn off.

## Go paperless

It's pretty standard nowadays to get all of your bank statements online, receipts emailed to you and bills in your personal account online. Avoiding this paper can add up over time to save lots of trees!

## Refuse unethical and unsustainable brands

Once you start to learn where the things you buy come from, it will become easier to say no to brands that aren't committed to being transparent about where they source their materials and who makes their products. It isn't always possible to only buy from completely ethical and sustainable companies, and all of us have fast fashion in our wardrobes, and products from unethical companies in our homes. But when and where you can, refuse companies that aren't doing well enough. Later in the book I will discuss in more detail about how you can say no to fast fashion, animal products and toxic chemicals.

❋

# Checklist of things you can refuse now:

○ .................................................................................

○ .................................................................................

○ .................................................................................

○ .................................................................................

○ .................................................................................

○ .................................................................................

○ .................................................................................

○ .................................................................................

○ .................................................................................

○ .................................................................................

○ .................................................................................

○ .................................................................................

○ .................................................................................

# Reduce

If you can't refuse, then reduce. Being smart about your purchases, making sure that you need them and that they'll last a long time, saves so many items from ending up in landfill. If refusal isn't an option, then reduction is the next best thing. This goes for anything from fast fashion to animal products to plastic-wrapped food. We can't always refuse, so reducing is still a big step.

## Cut down on plastic

Eliminating plastic altogether is a difficult task, so cut down as much as is feasible for you. Find alternatives to products that have excessive plastic. Think about the products you buy regularly that are packaged in or made from plastic, and start buying them less often by seeking out sustainable alternatives.

## Buy in bulk

Some shops now offer refill stations where you can fill up your own containers with food such as rice, pasta and legumes. If this isn't available near you, buy your groceries in bulk at your supermarket, especially on items you use a lot of, e.g. spices, grains or condiments. This often can end up cheaper, as well as saving on extra packaging.

## Shop local

Shopping locally not only supports the community you live in, but saves energy and waste from the journey of the product you're buying. Find local grocers or farmers' markets that grow food locally to you, and see if there are independent shops that hand-make products you would usually buy in a supermarket, high-street store or online. You will often find great bargains, feel a sense of community from getting to know smaller businesses, and local businesses usually use a lot less plastic than the big guys.

## Don't throw away your food

Around one-third of all food produced is wasted.[9] In the UK in 2017 the average household threw away £470 in food.[10] So ask yourself how much food you're binning each week. If you have leftover food, store it for the next day; if food is about to go off, freeze it; meal plan and meal prep to avoid food waste; don't over-purchase on foods you won't eat (don't shop when you're hungry – this gets me every time!). Try a freezer or pantry challenge to use up some food you already have.

## Buy secondhand

Secondhand is always the most sustainable option, and often the cheapest too! So if you need something, try to source it secondhand first. Whether that's clothing, electronics, furniture, gifts, anything! My favourite places to shop secondhand are charity and vintage shops, Facebook Marketplace, eBay, Depop and Gumtree. It can take time and patience, but is always worth it when you find a bargain that you're saving from landfill!

## Use menstrual cups/reusable pads

If you have a period, opting for reusable or more eco options can make a significant difference to your personal waste. You can switch to a menstrual cup, get reusable pads, tampon applicators, organic tampons or period underwear. I personally haven't looked back since switching to a menstrual cup. Periods are very personal to each person, so try out the different reusable options and find which one works for you!

## Make it last

Buy things that will last you a long time. Don't be tempted by the latest smartphone upgrade, or the newest pair of trainers. If what you have already is working, keep it and make it last. This starts with buying good-quality items, continues with taking care of what we own, and ends with avoiding the temptation for constant upgrades.

## Grow your own food

Use your garden (or even a windowsill) and grow your own veg! Things like herbs or potatoes are super easy to grow and it's the truest definition of eating local. You'll be delighted when you reap the rewards of the harvest in the next season.

## Go on a budget

Going on a budget can really help you to avoid impulse spending on things that may end up in landfill. Lowering your budget will inevitably lower your consumption. So go over that budget we discussed in the last chapter and stick to it to eliminate non-essential spending as much as possible. Go through your accounts for the last month or two, and see where you might be spending your money on wasteful things without realising it. Compare this to your monthly income, aiming to adjust your budget so that you are in a surplus rather than a deficit.

## Write down five ways you can reduce your waste:

What wasteful things do you buy regularly that you could reduce? Is there an easy swap that could be made, if not every time, but sometimes?

PLASTIC-WRAPPED SANDWICHES FROM THE SUPERMARKET ›
HOMEMADE SANDWICHES

1

2

3

4

5

# Reuse and Repurpose

The next step is to look at what we already have, and whether it can be reused or repurposed in some way. Here are ten easy ways to reuse items:

1   REUSABLE CONTAINERS, CUPS, BOTTLES, BAGS
    AND CUTLERY

    If you're refusing single-use plastic, then you'll need to bring your own! You don't necessarily have to go out and buy these things, as you probably already have some of them in your home that you can use out and about. Bring cutlery from your kitchen, old Tupperware, or that tote bag that came free with something you bought years ago. You can also invest in some great reusables such as travel sets of cutlery, metal straws, produce bags and coffee cups to take with you everywhere you go.

2   GLASS JARS, ALUMINIUM CANS AND PLASTIC
    CONTAINERS

    Old food jars, tins and plastic containers are perfect for storing pantry items, to organise things on your desk or as storage in your bedroom. There are so many ways you can reuse jars and containers around your home, such as making a tin of baked beans into a pen pot, turning old wine bottles into candle holders, or using recycled plastic containers to separate electronics in your desk drawer.

3   NEWSPAPERS, MAGAZINES AND PAPER

    These can make really unique gift-wrapping paper, you can shred it to use for hamsters or other small pets, to package things when moving home, or save it to soak up spills.

4   PACKAGING

    Any excess packaging you have from online orders can be reused to post your own things, to store fragile items in the attic, or for when you next move house.

5   CLOTHES, TOWELS AND BED LINEN

Old fabric items don't need to be thrown away as they can be
reused in so many ways! If they're still in good condition, they
can also be passed on to a charity shop, animal or homeless
shelter. If not, cut them up for use as cleaning rags, or as towels
for pets. Tying together odd socks can make great dogs' toys, bed
linen can be used as rags for your next home DIY project, and
sentimental T-shirts can be sewn together to form a memory-
filled blanket or rug.

6   PLASTIC BAGS

I'm not just talking plastic bags from your local supermarket,
but from any shop. Smaller bags can be washed, dried and used
as sandwich or food bags (just use a bag clip). If you have a dog,
take the bags with you on your walk to clean up their poo. Store
things in them around the home. Use them as stuffing when
posting packages. Donate to your local charity shop. Or simply
use them until they break for your grocery shopping!

7   BROKEN DISHES

If you accidentally smash your favourite mug or a dinner plate,
don't just throw it out. It can be used at the base of plant pots,
added to the compost in your garden, or if your mug has only
just lost the handle, it could be used as a cup to store pens,
hair-ties, and other miscellaneous items.

8   OLD OR BROKEN FURNITURE

Try repairing or upcycling your old furniture before taking
it down the dump, or sell it online so someone can enjoy it.
It's surprising how much a fresh layer of paint, or some new
handles, screws and varnishing can do for worn-out furniture.
If it's beyond repair, disassemble the materials to repurpose it
into something new. I once upcycled an old wardrobe door into
a desk by sanding, staining and attaching some legs. Wood can
be used to make shelves, and MDF can be used for photography
boards or as a canvas for an art project.

9　HOUSEHOLD DECOR

If a plant is dying, compost it or try planting it outside. Old
paintings can be reframed to appear more modern. Cushions
can be re-stuffed, or given a new cover altogether made from
some of your old bed linen or clothes. If you find any small
trinkets, these can be attached to a gift with the wrapping paper.
Keep nice boxes for storage. Spray-paint old mugs, containers
or empty candles to make them appear new again. Old lamps
can be painted, fixed with new bulbs or given a new lampshade
instead of buying a whole new lamp.

10 BOOKS

If you're done with a book it can be passed on to friends, your
local library, charity shop or school. But if they're falling apart,
try using them as decoration in your home. The paper inside can
be ripped out and used for wrapping paper or in art projects.
You could even make a cool tabletop by gluing layers of the
paper to the surface and varnish to protect it.

11 ELECTRONICS

Electronics quickly become obsolete, or out of date with the
latest technology, meaning we have to replace them more often
than we'd like to. Not only that, but advertising leads us to
believe we always need the latest tech. As you declutter you'll
find lots of old phones, wires and electronics lurking in drawers
and cupboards that you can get rid of. If you're upgrading or no
longer using a piece of electronics that is worth money, try to
sell it on. Otherwise, ask any friends if they want it, or donate it
for free. If it's beyond repair, there are other ways to repurpose.
Old wires can be used to tie things together. Old headphones or
cameras could be used for decoration.

✳

# Write down at least three things you want to reuse or repurpose in your home:

1 ............................................................................................

2 ............................................................................................

3 ............................................................................................

............................................................................................

............................................................................................

............................................................................................

............................................................................................

............................................................................................

............................................................................................

# Recycle

If all else fails and you haven't been able to reduce or reuse, then recycling is your next best option. The last place we want things to end up is in landfill. Most of the waste we produce ends up in there, so make it your absolute last resort to put something in the bin. Here are my top tips for recycling your waste.

## Create a system

Making it easy for you to recycle at home will make it a lot more likely that you'll recycle as much of your waste as possible. Most local councils will collect general recycling (plastics, paper, cardboard, glass, cans) outside your home, so separate your rubbish into different bins/bags ready for collection. Keep these recycling containers next to your main bin as a reminder each time you throw something away. Challenge yourself to fill your recycling bins up faster than your rubbish/landfill bin.

## Wash, then recycle

Always wash any items that you're sending to recycling. Recycling centres won't accept soiled bottles, containers or packaging that is covered in food or product, and they may therefore end up in landfill.

## Recycle more

Look beyond your usual recyclable items such as plastic water bottles, tin cans and glass:

- toilet paper rolls
- tin foil
- empty plastic toiletry bottles
- electric wires
- wrapping paper
- birthday cards

- plastic food trays and bags
- crisp packets
- laundry detergent bottles: anything that has a recyclable material (paper, plastic, metal, glass) has the potential to be recycled.

Take packaging apart, sort the recycling and don't be lazy with throwing certain items in the bin that could be recycled. Most packaging will have a symbol to indicate if it can be recycled or not.

If certain items aren't collected from your home with the other recycling, such as plastic bags/wrappers, then collect these items to take to your local recycling centre or supermarket. Plastic carrier bags, plastic wrap, bread bags, clear food bags, frozen vegetable packets can all be taken to your supermarket to be recycled (just make sure they don't have any leftover food in them and are clean).

## Learn

Knowledge is power. If you are unsure about what can or can't be recycled, then dig deeper and find out. Call up your local recycling centre, phone the company that owns the product you're trying to recycle, or do some research online. Learning what *can't* be recycled is also another way to understand what materials and items to try to avoid. For example, Styrofoam, bubble wrap, aerosol cans, medical needles, paper towels and pizza boxes are just some items that can't be recycled.

## Compost

If you aren't composting already, the weight of your rubbish bin is likely coming from all of the food waste. There is a common misconception that if you put your food in the bin, it will decompose at landfill. Unfortunately when food waste goes to landfill, it breaks down anaerobically, producing methane which is a harmful greenhouse gas. If you compost your food separately, however, carbon dioxide is created instead as part of the carbon cycle, and is therefore a lot less harmful. You're basically putting the food back into the earth in a nice little circle. You can compost in your garden easily, but there are many other ways to compost in your own home. See pages 248–251 for a full guide to composting.

### Recycle at school and work

If your school or work isn't recycling already, set something in place to make your efforts go further. As these are areas where lots of people spend their time, you can help to save a lot of unnecessary waste, all the while educating and influencing those around you to be more waste-conscious. Encourage your school or workplace to start composting food waste in the cafeteria, or to use recycling bins around the school/office. Have a conversation with someone in charge, get people to sign a petition and make it happen!

### Take it home

Make sure not to leave your principles at the door when you leave your house. If there aren't recycling facilities when you're out and about, take your recyclable materials home with you to recycle there. I always try to take home glass or plastic bottles if there isn't a recycling bin when I'm out.

### Dispose of things properly

If you're getting rid of your electrical items, such as an old fridge, air conditioner, computer, printer, cooker, old phone, then make sure to do it properly. These can contain harmful chemicals and materials that we don't want to end up in our atmosphere or environment. If they're still usable, sell or find a new home for them. If they can't be sold, make sure to dispose of them responsibly by calling up your local council or recycling centre for advice.

After doing some research by looking online or calling the relevant organisations and people, make yourself a handy list of what can and can't be recycled easily and locally.

## What can be recycled:

(and where)

## What can't be recycled:

(and I therefore can be mindful of buying in the future/ can find alternatives to or ways to repurpose myself)

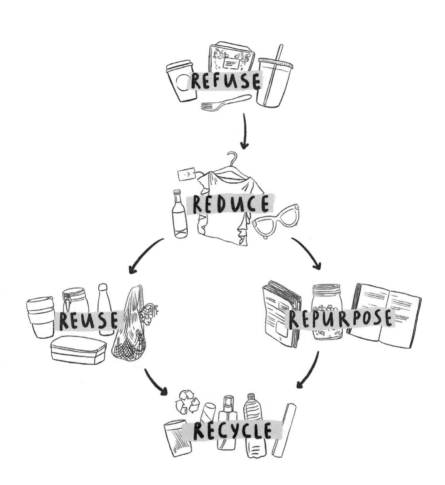

# How to Get in Touch About Waste and Climate Change

I strongly encourage you to become more involved in this conversation, put pressure on governments and your local MP to vote for green policies, and spend your money supporting companies who are leading the way for sustainability and reducing waste. Climate change, plastic and waste are all closely linked to politics, advertising and economics. Business has been put above the health of the Earth for a long time now, and not enough is happening to make large companies accountable.

1   Email or meet with your local representative (Member of Parliament or Congress, etc.) to tell them you care about the environment and the current climate emergency*.

2   Ask them what they're doing to reduce plastic, greenhouse gases and waste.

3   Tell them that if they want your vote, they need to put forward green policies and react *now* to the climate crisis.

4   Get a group of friends and family involved who also care, put together a petition from your neighbours, your school friends or work colleagues and bring it to your local representative. We need to be vocal to influence those in power, so do not hesitate to make your voices heard. They are there to represent us, our concerns, needs and wants.

I also recommend you do a little bit of research about your local representative to find out what positions they hold, so you can relate to their passions and find a way to make them understand your point of view. You can find out this information from the link provided below, or by searching their name on Google, YouTube or Twitter to hear what they've been up to. This isn't an opportunity to fight against their views, but a chance to make them sympathetic to yours.

* If you're in the UK, find out who your local MP is at www.theyworkforyou.com

# Sustainability, Guilt and Health

One of the huge downsides to reducing your waste and becoming more environmentally aware is how depressing facing the state our world is in can be sometimes. What we are doing to our beautiful planet, and the animals, creatures and plants we share it with, is absolutely devastating. It's easy to become overwhelmed by it all and want to just stick our heads in the sand, never to think about it again. Eco anxiety is being talked about more and more and we increasingly fear for our future. Caring for the planet is time-consuming, and trying to fight against an unsustainable system is tiring.

But we mustn't get bogged down by the world's problems, and instead we must focus on what we can do to help. The more of us that make individual changes and the more of us that speak up, the better. We must keep fighting by reducing our individual impact and spreading the word. We have to make our voices heard by our families, friends, brands and governments so that we can stop the worst from happening.

How we do this is therefore important. As much as we mustn't harshly judge others, we also mustn't harshly judge ourselves. Facing up to the realities of your personal carbon footprint can be empowering rather than something to be ashamed of. Maybe you had to buy a bottle of water in another country because the tap water isn't safe to drink. Maybe you are using lots of single-use plastic every day as part of your medication. Maybe you fly regularly for work or to visit family. Maybe you buy food wrapped in plastic because it's cheaper and you're on a budget. Maybe you ordered a drink and it came with a straw without you knowing ... I could list so many more examples of times when we aren't 'sustainable'. But is it our fault? Or is it because our systems are set up to be unsustainable?

We can't break down what is and isn't 'sustainable' to a simple set of criteria we aim to tick off. It isn't black and white. It isn't a one size fits all. It isn't as simple as knowing something isn't environmentally friendly and giving it up in an instant. Everyone's lives are different and everyone starts from a different place – not to mention that different levels of mental health, physical health, economic status or even our personalities can decide how well we can cope with these lifestyle changes. If you're making changes and aiming to improve, then that's what matters.

People put me on a pedestal as someone who speaks up about veganism, minimalism and sustainability online. However, I am far from the perfect vegan, minimalist or environmentalist. It took me time to go vegan and understand how to adapt my eating habits, especially as someone whose recovery from an eating disorder and going vegan coincided. Similarly, to this day, I still buy things that I regret buying, and that I end up decluttering. I still fly because it's more affordable and less time-consuming. I have areas where I want to do better, but I remember not to expect these changes overnight. My actions have changed so much over the years that I know from experience the time it takes to make these changes.

There are so many hurdles we have to overcome during this process, so remain kind to yourself. Make this an empowering process so that these sustainable switches actually *are* sustainable for you. The last thing we need is loads of people trying to be 100 per cent vegan and 100 per cent zero waste (both of which are practically impossible), and throwing in the towel within the year because it caused them more stress than it was worth. We need everyone to do what they can do, within their *own* personal limits, to make a collective difference.

So how about we focus on each other's strengths, and come together to make a change? We can't *all* do it all. There are activists out there, speaking up about the environment, campaigning and protesting to pressure our governments to change. There are scientists researching and coming up with new technology to help our environment. There are entrepreneurs starting sustainable and ethical businesses. And there are people at home making small changes in their daily lives and influencing those around them. Find out what your strength is, do what you can, and be a part of change.

※

# What three changes have I made in my life to be more sustainable or to reduce my waste?

(what impact has this had on my life, those around
me and potentially the environment?)

1 ....................................................................................

....................................................................................

2 ....................................................................................

....................................................................................

3 ....................................................................................

....................................................................................

# What three ways do I want to further reduce my waste in the future, and what impact will this have?

1 ....................................................................................

....................................................................................

2 ....................................................................................

....................................................................................

3 ....................................................................................

....................................................................................

# three

—

# wardrobe and fashion

# Fast Fashion

If you're reading this book opposite a wardrobe brimming with clothes from fast-fashion outlets, or you're waiting on an order from one of them to be delivered to your door this week, then don't worry, I've been there.

I used to live for recreating the looks I'd seen in *Vogue* and *Elle* with cheaper alternatives. Part of it was artistic expression and a bit of fun, but the other side was the pressure to be relevant and beautiful. I got carried away with spending my money and placing far too much importance on what I owned as a representation of who I was. Magazines and other media have so many of us hooked on the idea that you need to dress a certain way in order to be cool or important.

I regularly stayed up late at night scrolling every fast–fashion outlet hunting for the perfect outfit to wear for my next night out. I lived for the weekends when I could go shopping with friends and buy the latest trends. I worked long hours, sometimes at multiple jobs, in order to fund my shopaholic tendencies. A huge part of my identity was being the 'fashionable one' – fashion was everything to me. But it wasn't making me happy, and it was only acting as a distraction from bigger problems.

I never really stopped to think about where the clothes I was hoarding were coming from or the impact my shopping habit had on myself, as well as the planet and other people. This was until I learnt more about fast fashion. I realised I needed to stop wasting my money, and I learnt about how harmful the fashion industry is. Luckily after quitting fast fashion, my obsession for secondhand shopping was enough to maintain my shopping addiction for a while. I soon curtailed these habits, and swapped shopping for decluttering. Now I tend to only shop for clothing a couple of times a year, sticking to secondhand or sustainably and ethically made clothes.

The fashion industry is a harmful one. Not only can it affect our confidence and bank balances, but it is damaging to the planet and the people who are making our clothes. With most fast-fashion brands producing over 50 new collections every year, this business model is highly profitable, but highly unsustainable. Such a high rate of production unfortunately comes at a cost. Turning over this many clothes can mean workers aren't paid sufficiently or treated ethically, while shocking amounts of waste is produced and devastating harm is done to the environment.

The way in which fashion is produced has dramatically changed in recent years. Fast-fashion retailers are producing small amounts of stock very often, encouraging consumers to come back regularly to buy stuff. The feeling that you have to make sure you grab something quickly before it sells out wasn't something that would go through people's minds a few decades ago. This profitable but unsustainable business model is making brands more money than ever, as they have sold us all on the idea of disposable fashion. We don't keep clothes for as long as we used to, and we're drawn in by the constant newness, replacing last season's 'unfashionable' clothes with this season's latest new trend. This throwaway culture means that we'd rather get rid of something and replace it with something cheap and new, than repair it.

If we want to change the impact of fashion, not only does this business model need to change, but so do our own attitudes towards buying clothing.

## Waste and the environment

The fashion industry is shockingly damaging to the environment. High levels of water and toxic pesticides are used in the process of growing materials like cotton, and the toxic dyes that make our clothes the latest fashionable colours are the second largest polluter of clean water globally, after agriculture.[11] The synthetic fibres in our clothes are carbon intensive as they require oil to be made, and take hundreds, if not thousands, of years to biodegrade. Those tiny microfibres often end up in the ocean when we wash the clothes in our washing machine. The global fashion industry is one of the leading contributors to climate change, producing 1.2 billion tonnes of carbon emissions in 2015.[12]

Then there's the waste. As a consequence of fast fashion, three in five garments end up in landfill or incinerators within a year, as more and more people are tempted to constantly buy new trendy items for their wardrobes.[13] Brands are even destroying their unsold clothes and accessories in a bid to protect their brand exclusivity, with Burberry famously incinerating £28.6 million worth in 2017.[14] We are buying more and more clothes than ever before, twice as many items of clothing than we did a decade ago, resulting in 235 million items of clothing being sent to landfill in 2017.[15]

As our population grows, and the fashion industry continues their unsustainable habits, these numbers are only set to rise over the next decade.

## Human rights

In order to keep up with demand, garment workers around the world are being mistreated in order to make fast fashion. To keep profits high and costs down, it makes sense for brands to choose factories who offer the cheapest price. The catch? Some of these factories are cutting corners on health and safety, and slashing wages, in order to remain competitive. This can lead to exploitation, abuse and discrimination against workers. People in countries such as India, Indonesia and Cambodia aren't being paid enough to meet the basic necessities of life, just so we can fuel our need for new and cheap clothes.

Unfortunately a lack of transparency is apparent across the board from fast-fashion retailers who fail to reveal the details of their supply chain. These hidden trade secrets have allowed consumers to buy without guilt for far too long. However, people are wising up to what is going on, and becoming more and more inquisitive about where their clothes come from.

## Animal products

Many fast-fashion brands still use wool, fur and leather in their products, and are sourcing them unethically. These materials often come from factory farms where there is little to no regard for the wellbeing of animals or the effects on the environment.[16] The waste created from the fur and leather industries contaminate the surrounding water with dangerous and toxic substances, and the hazardous processes used also heavily pollute the air.[17] Not only this, but the health of those working in these factories is jeopardised by being exposed to this pollution.[18] The wool industry is no better, as sheep encounter cruel practices to meet the high demand for the material[19], and their farming deteriorates the land and soil and decreases biodiversity, while consuming and polluting huge amounts of water.[20]

Due to this wide array of issues posed by animal agriculture, more sustainable and ethical alternatives are popping up and gaining popularity. It's therefore becoming easier for us to say no to animal ingredients used in fast fashion. Some great sustainable and renewable fabrics are organic hemp, cotton, bamboo or linen. There are also new and innovative alternatives to leather that look and feel just like it, made from pineapples, cork and mushrooms. But since some of those alternatives can be expensive or inaccessible, the next best option is to shop secondhand or vintage. That way you can wear wool and leather, without contributing to its demand.

## Slow fashion

What's the alternative? Slow, sustainable and ethical fashion! Shop less, love the clothes you own, opt for secondhand instead of new, buy from small independent designers and support companies that are committed to sustainable practices such as only bringing out a few new collections per year, using sustainable fabrics, and paying their workers fair wages in safe working conditions.

As Vivienne Westwood once said, 'Buy less. Choose well. Make it last.'

Most importantly, slow fashion is about re-evaluating our own relationship with fashion, by appreciating the clothes we already own, taking care of them and finding new ways to wear them. Only buy new clothes when we genuinely need them, opting for better quality fabrics, and trying our best to source them responsibly.

Slowing down when it comes to fashion is a lifelong process. You probably have some fast fashion in your wardrobe, and it doesn't need to be replaced with ethical brands or sustainable materials. That in itself isn't sustainable. So use the things you love, and be mindful with any purchases you make from now on. This will take time, and you'll learn more as you go.

Thankfully, in the past few years sustainability within the fashion industry is a growing trend, making it easier to find brands and creators committed to providing clothing that doesn't hide any dirty secrets, and more places for us to easily get secondhand fashion. There has been a significant increase in people looking to buy responsibly-sourced fashion, with a 66 per cent increase in searches for sustainable fashion since 2018.[21]

Where's a good place to start? Our wardrobes.

# Decluttering Your Wardrobe

The process of decluttering your wardrobe can help you to understand your style, create a wardrobe of key pieces you can wear over and over, and make better decisions about what clothes you buy in the future. If you learn to love your wardrobe, you're a lot less likely to feel the need to impulse buy.

So rope a friend in, try *everything* on, look in the mirror and be honest about what you do and don't wear.

### Questions to ask yourself:

- Does it give me confidence?
- Is it good quality/condition?
- Does it fit me well?
- Is it easy to pair with other items in my wardrobe?
- Is it comfortable?
- Do I wear it regularly (in the last 3–6 months)?
- Does it fit my lifestyle?

### Things to think about:

- What colours do I like wearing?
- What styles do I enjoy?
- What clothes make me feel like me?
- What items do I keep going back to again and again?
- How do I spend my time, and how do my clothes fit these lifestyle habits?
- What do I *need* to wear for the jobs, hobbies and activities I do?
- What do I *want* to wear to feel my best?

Our clothing can be the hardest to declutter, so refer back to Chapter 1 to go over these steps in detail if you haven't already. This process of decluttering should help you to re-evaluate your relationship with fashion, be more appreciative of the clothes you own, and face up to some regrettable fashion choices you've made in the past. Keep the above questions and thoughts in your mind, and be honest with your answers to help you in the process of downsizing your wardrobe.

# Mend your clothes!

- Iron-on patches. Use these if your jeans rip. No sewing machine needed!
- Stitch up holes with a simple needle and thread sewing kit. It's easy to do and can save a hole from getting any larger.
- Stained? Soak in warm soapy water to get out the stain before it sets, and hopefully your clothes will come out good as new.
- Get a family member or friend to help if you don't know how to sew, or take it somewhere to be repaired.

## ① CHOOSE AN AREA

### CATEGORY

DRESSES
JUMPERS/SWEATERS/CARDIGANS
TOPS/SHIRTS
BOTTOMS
PLAYSUITS/JUMPSUITS/DUNGAREES
JACKET/COATS
SHOES
BAGS
PYJAMAS AND LOUNGEWEAR
ACCESSORIES
ACTIVEWEAR
UNDERWEAR/SOCKS/SWIMWEAR

### AREA

CHEST OF DRAWERS
WARDROBE
SHELVES
CUPBOARD
STORAGE BOXES

## ② TAKE EVERYTHING OUT

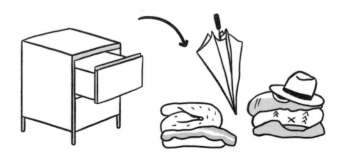

# Creating a Curated and Capsule Closet

Decluttering can be a difficult process. You want to keep things that hold sentimental value, clothes that you wore once that made you feel incredible, and items that you hope to fit into one day for that special event. But you have to allow yourself to let go of these things. It's surprising how quickly you'll forget about them once you have made the choice to get rid of them. So if you aren't wearing it or it doesn't fit, let it go. Sentimental items can be particularly hard, so take the time to appreciate the clothes and the memories they hold, but ask yourself whether keeping them hidden in a drawer is necessary to keep these memories. You'll know in your heart if it's time to say goodbye or not.

You may have heard of ideas such as 'Project 333', where for three months you only wear 33 items of clothing. For many this is a great way to figure out what items in your wardrobe you do or don't wear, and to realise that you don't need as much as you once thought you did. Similarly lots of people try to own less than a specific number of clothes, such as owning under 50 items of clothing or under 25. These are great initiatives to get you going with your capsule wardrobe; however, if they don't appeal to you, do it your own way – after all, your wardrobe, your rules! All of these projects and rules come from the same idea of owning less and being more mindful with your wardrobe choices. Even if the suggestions I've made in this book don't suit you, find a way that does.

After culling your clothes, you're likely to see patterns, colours, shapes and styles repeated throughout your wardrobe. You might be someone who gravitates towards neutral cool tones, or someone who likes patterns and bright colours. Have a look at your wardrobe as a whole, and notice what colours and styles are common. This will make it easier to put together outfits and buy clothes in the future. Reducing what you own to matching and complementary styles, colour palettes and shapes will not only save you time getting dressed in the mornings, but enable you to dress like *you*.

## Refresher declutter

Twice a year (or more), do a refresher declutter of your clothes.
Go through everything again, reorganise and consider what
clothes you haven't been wearing, you've grown out of or that
are worn out.

## Separating seasons

After you've decluttered, separate your things into seasons.
Think about what you'll be wearing for the cold or warm
months ahead. Winter clothes, such as fluffy jumpers, and
summer clothes, such as bikinis, can be stored away for next
year. This not only frees up space in your wardrobe, but makes
it a lot easier for you to pick outfits and make the most of your
clothes. Plus each season, you have the benefit of feeling like
you've gained a whole new wardrobe!

## Colour palette

Many minimalists gravitate towards neutral colours such as
blacks, greys and whites. This is often because these tones are
simple and versatile. If, like me, you enjoy wearing colours then
find the colours you love, and think about this palette when
buying clothes. As you downsize you will notice which colours
your wardrobe has the most of, and which make you feel your
best. Having a few key tones in your capsule wardrobe will
make it easy for you to mix and match your outfits.

## Fewer items

A capsule wardrobe has a limited number of items that you are
able to coordinate in many different ways. This can be a really
considered approach where you count the items you own to
form a variety of outfits for all occasions. Or if you're like me
and prefer a more relaxed approach, consider how much you
own and try to keep it to only what you love. Less truly is more.
A successful capsule wardrobe is simply one that offers you
everything you personally need, and no more.

## Basics

Owning basics that can go with a variety of other key pieces is essential. To keep it simple, you may want your entire wardrobe to be made up of only basics. Comfy T-shirts, well-fitting jeans, smart trousers, a sturdy backpack and a versatile pair of shoes are some great examples of basics that can be paired with other complementary pieces to create a variety of outfits.

## Long-lasting essentials

The approach to your wardrobe should move towards quality over quantity. If you aren't spending so much money on cheap fast fashion, you might be able to save up for items made from higher-quality materials that will stand the test of time. Funnily enough, most of the clothes that have remained in my wardrobe for years are the ones I've bought secondhand. These items were typically of higher quality than the cheaper fast fashion I was buying new. Long-lasting doesn't need to cost the earth!

## Key pieces and shapes

Everyone has a different body type, lifestyle and personal style. Downsizing can tell us what shapes we find the most flattering and enjoyable to wear. Keep this in mind when curating your wardrobe, and don't make the mistake of buying items in the future you like the idea of, more than you like on your body. Know what suits you and makes you feel your best. These key styles can be repeated throughout your wardrobe for an easy and long-lasting way of dressing.

## Style-driven over trend-driven

Now you've found your personal style, don't be tempted by trends that you love on other people, that realistically you just aren't going to wear. Keep in mind the style that feels like you, and avoid buying fashionable clothes and accessories that just don't live up to their hype.

# Finding Your Minimalist Style

There is not a particular way that a minimalist's wardrobe should look. Whether you love neutrals or colour, live in summer clothes or own different things for different seasons, it doesn't matter. What does matter is that you become more aware of what you own in order to create a capsule wardrobe that fits your lifestyle.

## Keep what you love

It's pretty easy to know what clothes you love in your wardrobe: the things you wear day in day out, and the clothes that make you feel confident and beautiful. By getting rid of the rest, your favourite clothes will be centre stage for you to pick out and wear each day. It's a lot easier to choose an outfit from a smaller collection of all of your favourite clothes, than a bigger wardrobe filled with lots of clothes. I enjoy my wardrobe a lot more now that I have decluttered and found my own style. Rediscover items that have been hidden that you would love to wear more often, and get enjoyment from rewearing outfits that make you feel your best.

## Enjoy what you have

In pursuit of the perfect capsule wardrobe, it can be tempting to want to go out and buy a whole new one. But stick with what you already have for a little while, only adding one or two pieces if you need to. Appreciating the clothes you already own and finding new ways to style them will help you understand what works for you. Discover new ways to style old clothes. And have fun with it!

# How to Be a Sustainable Shopper

### Shop less

Shopping less is the simplest and most direct way that you can have an impact on your carbon footprint when it comes to fashion. The less you buy, the less you're supporting the linear and unsustainable economy of fast fashion. Replace old shopping habits with a more mindful approach to what you're adding to your wardrobe.

### Find the why

We've discussed how finding the 'why' can help when it comes to minimalism, but it can apply to anything you want to do in life. You need to figure out why you are setting yourself this goal in order to fulfil it. Why do you want to stop shopping? To reduce your carbon footprint? To save money or to clear your debt? To spend that money on more useful or meaningful things? For a tidier home? All of the above?

## Write down anything that will motivate you in this process:

..................................................................................................

..................................................................................................

..................................................................................................

..................................................................................................

..................................................................................................

## Think before you buy

Clothing can be a huge weakness for many of us.

Note these questions in your phone to quickly look over every time you're tempted to buy new clothes. And be honest and ruthless with your answers.

- Do I need it?
- Do I love it?
- Am I happy with my current wardrobe?
- Is this item versatile?
- Does it make me feel amazing?
- Does the colour and style fit with what I already own?
- Can I think of at least three different outfits I can create with my existing clothes?
- Do I already own something similar that is enough?
- Will I wear it a lot?
- Could I borrow it from a friend instead?
- Is it trendy, rather than my personal style?

## One in, one out

The one in, one out rule is perfect to stop things from accumulating in your home. Every time you go to buy something, find something at home that you can declutter. Sell an item of clothing you've been meaning to get rid of, and use this money towards your new purchase. Not only will this stop you buying things you don't need, but it will maintain your decluttering efforts!

## Would you buy it if it was more expensive?

This question is a great way to stop yourself from buying things that are cheap or on sale just for the sake of it. I used to be a sucker for getting bargains at cheap fast-fashion brands and charity shops just because they were cheap. Great deals trick us into getting things we just don't need. There is nothing wrong with a good ol' bargain, but just make sure it's worth it!

### Find a new positive habit

Replace your shopping habit with something positive. This could be sport, reading, learning a new skill, yoga, writing, pursuing your dream career, meditation, gardening – literally anything that makes you happy and doesn't have any negative impact on your life. The times that you would usually spend shopping, fill it with a new productive or fun hobby!

### Declutter your life

When you start to declutter, it makes it more difficult to bring new things into your life. Once you experience a clean wardrobe, shopping for new stuff feels counterintuitive. I honestly get the same kick from decluttering that I once got from shopping. Next time you get the urge, get up and start decluttering somewhere around the house!

### Remove temptation

I'm sure you can pinpoint people, websites or brands that regularly tempt you into buying new clothes. Maybe a friend you always go shopping with, or a newsletter you're subscribed to that alerts you to the latest sales. Whatever gets you scrolling fast-fashion websites late at night, you've got to get rid of it. Unsubscribe, unfollow and delete. Arrange to go for lunch with your friends instead of shopping, or do a fun outdoor activity. Make a point of removing any temptation that could possibly creep in and ruin your good intentions.

### Borrow

Next time you have a big night out, or a hot date, ask a friend and borrow something! You might need an entire outfit, or just a nice jacket to complement something you already own. If you think you'd be buying something only to wear it once, borrowing is the answer! I often do this by raiding my sister's or best friends' wardrobes. It's a bit of fun, and you can offer to return the favour next time they need a new outfit!

# Shop Secondhand

Now you've regained some control of your shopping habits, if you do want to buy something, try to find it secondhand instead of new first. Aim to get most of your clothing and accessories secondhand.

If it has already been made, it's not only way more affordable, but it saves a lot of resources. There are so many clothes already out there, just waiting to be loved. The thrill you get from finding a hidden gem for a bargain price always beats shopping on the high street. It can take a little more effort, however, hopefully with my help, you'll be an expert in secondhand fashion in no time.

## Places to secondhand shop

1  CHARITY/THRIFT SHOPS

One of the easiest ways to secondhand shop is to visit your local town and head into a charity or thrift shop. Visit a few and find your favourites, as they will vary in price and quality. One of my best tips is to visit affluent areas, as these typically have higher-quality clothes and, if you're lucky, expensive designer items. And the best part about charity shops is that the money for your purchase goes to a good cause, so hunt out charities that you'd like to support.

2  VINTAGE SHOPS

These are great places to source things such as denim, coats and jackets, shoes, accessories, summer dresses and unique items. They are usually pricier than a charity or thrift shop, as someone has collected and curated the items for you to shop. However, you can still find affordable vintage shops if you do some hunting. My favourite part about vintage shopping is finding something that is totally unique that you would never be able to buy new – something that has a story and history behind it.

3 FACEBOOK SELLING SITES

Another favourite place I love to shop secondhand is on
Facebook. Delve into their Marketplace or join a local selling
site in your area (to find this, type in your local towns and then
add 'selling site' and hopefully your area will have one), and start
searching! This can take some scrolling, but with patience you
can get some amazing bargains locally.

4 FASHION APPS

Fashion apps and sites dedicated to secondhand are sometimes
the best way to go. Some of the more popular places are eBay,
Depop, Poshmark, Thred Up and Vinted. Vestaire Collective
is also a great place to sell and buy secondhand luxury items.
What I love about these sites is that it makes it easy to search
for what you're specifically looking for, plus you can sell your
unwanted items on there too. With patience, I will be able to
find what I want, in my size, the colour I'm after, within a few
weeks of browsing these sites. You can save items, watch them
and make offers to get a great deal. It makes you realise just how
many unwanted clothes and accessories there are out there!
Secondhand fashion apps are also generally better for plus-sized
options as well as an overall easier shopping experience than
hunting through racks of clothing across multiple charity shops
on the high street!

5 CLOTHING SWAPS

Clothing swaps are a super fun and social way to get new
clothes without spending any money at all. If you've just done a
big clear out, organise a clothing swap with your friends where
you all bring your clothes together in one place and swap!
Recently there have been more and more organised events for
clothing swaps, so find out if there are any happening near to
you, or set one up yourself!

## My top tips

1 TRY EVERYTHING ON

So many times I've picked up over ten items from inside a charity shop, only to find out they fit awfully or look nothing like they did on the hanger. So, I always take the time to take them to the changing room. Some charity or thrift shops won't have a changing room, so dress in something you can easily slip clothes over in the shop to see if they fit.

2 COME PREPARED

Whenever I'm secondhand shopping I try to think of what I'm after beforehand. Saving styles and items you're after on Pinterest is a great way to do this. Maybe even look through your wardrobe and write a list. It helps to know what you're looking for when you're hunting through racks of assorted clothing, or scrolling through what's available on a secondhand clothing app. Not only this, but it minimises impulse decisions.

3 PRACTISE PATIENCE

Secondhand shopping isn't as quick as buying new. You can't easily get exactly what you need, in your size at the click of a button, delivered to your door. I find it very satisfying when I take the time to hunt something out, and end up finding what I'm after for a fraction of the price! Give it time, hunt around and you'll hopefully find what you're looking for.

4 SET A BUDGET

Just because something is cheap and affordable doesn't mean you should buy it. I used to fall into this trap by only shopping at charity shops because I was a broke student, but I ended up spending my entire food budget on multiple items I rarely wore. Stay on the safe side and bring cash to stick to a budget.

5 UNISEX SHOP

I have never been one to stick to the women's section of a charity shop or secondhand fashion apps. Men's jumpers, jackets, shirts, shoes and coats are often better than what the women's section has to offer!

6   ONLY BUY WHAT YOU LOVE

This applies to any form of shopping, but remember to only buy
what you absolutely love. If you're unsure whether it fits right, if
you have anything to wear it with, or where you'll wear it, then
leave it behind, no matter how cheap it is.

7   BARTER

If you're shopping on apps such as Depop, you can try to strike
up a deal with whoever you're buying from. Ask if they're open
to offers, or if you're buying multiple items, see if they'll give
you a reduced rate. Similarly on eBay you can send the seller a
private message to see if they'll take a 'buy it now' offer.

8   STICK TO CLASSICS

Classics will always stand the test of time, plus they're a lot easier
to find in a messy charity shop or vintage store. My favourite
items to look out for are coats, jumpers, denim, oversized shirts
and shoes. These are easy to spot, and a good starting point if
you ever feel overwhelmed in a secondhand shop.

9   CHECK MATERIALS

The label can indicate the longevity or quality of an item of
clothing. If it's made from natural, instead of synthetic, fibres this
will not only be better for the environment, but is often likely to
be of better quality. Natural fibres such as linen, hemp, bamboo,
organic cotton (conventional cotton is heavy on the pesticides)
are biodegradable, recyclable and gentle on your skin. Similarly,
check the labels to see what brands you're buying from. While
designer labels don't always mean something is higher quality,
they very often are. I also like to look out for vintage items, as
these are often of higher quality.

10 DONATE OR SELL WHILE YOU SHOP

Next time you go to a charity shop, trade something in before
you buy something new! This is a good way of making yourself
accountable for the things you're buying, as well as donating to
charity. Similarly if you're buying secondhand online, put something up for sale and use that money towards your purchase.

# Become a Detective

If you want to find out whether your favourite brand is sustainable or ethical, it's time to get your detective hat on.

### Price

If the clothes are very cheap, then it's likely the workers who made the clothes weren't paid fairly. Consider the journey of the item of clothing, including the different workers who designed the clothes, harvested the material, dyed it, cut it, sewed it, packaged it, shipped it and then sold it on your local high street. This doesn't even slightly cover the amount of people who went into producing that one single item of clothing. Does the price tag reasonably add up to paying all of these workers fairly?

### Quality

Does the item of clothing appear to be of good quality? Is it sewn well? Can you see discrepancies between the same item displayed in the shop? The poorer the quality, the cheaper it was to make and the less consideration was put into its production (and the sooner it will fall apart and have to be bought again).

### Collections

How many collections does this brand bring out a year? Do you see new clothing every time you go into the shop or check the website? If a brand is turning over multiple collections each season, then this is fast fashion that comes at a cost.

### Materials

Are most of the items from this brand made from cheap or synthetic materials? Do they use anything organic or recycled in their collections? If all you are seeing is polyester and non-organic natural materials, then it's likely this brand isn't making enough of an effort for their products to be more sustainable.

## Labels

Looking out for labels on clothing that are certified to ensure whether things are organic or fairtrade is a good way to find brands that are sourcing ethical and sustainable fabrics and products.

**Check the label for:**

- Organic
- GOTS (Global Organic Textile Standard certified)
- Fairtrade
- Fair Wear
- Vegan

## Google

Maybe it's obvious, but the first thing I always do when I want to know about a brand is do a quick Google search of the name of the brand followed by 'ethics' or 'sustainability'. Here you can find reviews and articles discussing the company and rating them on their values and commitments so that you can make an informed decision.

## Check the website

One of the best places you can look to find out about a company's ethics and sustainability values is on their website. A red flag is when you can't find any page about their line of production, their standards, the factories their clothes are made in, or the materials they're made from. Usually companies that pride themselves on their sustainability and ethics will make this very clear on their 'about' pages, or in the descriptions of their clothing.

## Diversity and variety

Look out for brands that are modelling their clothes on a diverse range of people in their marketing material, and is considering a wide range of shapes and sizes when making their clothing. Representation and inclusivity matter hugely.

## Questions to ask brands

If you are unsure about what a brand is doing behind the scenes, then get in touch! Send them an email or letter, or leave a comment on their social media asking them questions. Try to get an answer from them about the ethics and sustainability of their practices, and urge them to do better if it is evident to you that they aren't doing enough. If we all did this, maybe they'd start to listen.

- Do you pay your workers a living wage?
- Are your workers ever subject to discrimination, enslavement, exploitation, harassment or danger in the workplace?
- Is child labour used in your factories?
- Are the workers in the factories you use able to form unions to negotiate better working conditions?
- Do you recycle your materials or use recycled materials in your clothing lines?
- How long do you keep your clothes?
- Do you incinerate unsold or returned stock?
- What sustainable materials are you using or introducing into your product lines?
- How are you reducing the flow of microfibres into the sea?
- Do you credit all artists, designers and craftsmen for the designs of your clothing?
- As a brand are you inclusive to all race, class, gender, age, shape and ability?
- Do you have a variety of sizes, including plus size?

The answers to these questions should be clear, and we should be able to demand that they are made clear to us as a consumer.

The organisation Fashion Revolution has lots of great resources on their website to help you get in touch with brands and to ask that they're more transparent about their supply chain. They also release a downloadable fashion index that ranks 100 of the top fashion brands in the world on their transparency.

# Shop Ethical and Independent Brands

Now that you've done your research and begun to dig deeper into whether your favourite brands are ethical, it's time to find some brands out there you can rely on. I've completely changed the places I shop at and continue to see amazing brands popping up as sustainable and ethical fashion grows.

Where do you begin?

## Search

Start by finding out what is local to your country. Have a quick Google search to see what brands are creating fashion ethically and sustainably where you live. I always type in something like 'ethical brands UK', 'slow fashion brands', or maybe a more specific shop for 'ethical brands underwear', or 'sustainable shoes'. Ask around to see if anyone knows of any smaller brands, or independent designers or creators.

## Social media

Instagram is a great place to hunt for up-and-coming brands. I love following bloggers who shop sustainably and promote ethical fashion, looking at the brands they're tagging in their images and promoting. Social media is the new word of mouth, so make sure to follow some eco influencers.

## Local

As brands grow bigger, and start to sell further afield, corners are cut. This is why smaller and local designers and creators are often more sustainable and ethical. Visit your local town or city, markets or exhibitions, and hunt out small businesses. You can speak directly with these people about their clothes, how they're made and what they are made from. Smaller businesses rely on your money to keep going, and if we want slow and ethical fashion to become the norm, we have the power to make a shift with our wallets.

## Support BIPOC

Furthermore, buy from BIPOC (Black, Indigenous and People of Colour) creators, makers and fashion designers to support their long-standing work in the ethical and slow fashion community. Diversity is key to ethical fashion. Follow @buyfrombipoc to get involved and commit to purchasing from BIPOC creatives and sharing their work with your friends, family and online.

## Handmade

Look on social media and places such as Etsy for people who create handmade clothing from natural materials. They might not be an established brand or company, just someone earning a living making clothes.

## Give it time

By slowing down your consumption of fashion, you can allow the time to source brands that are transparent. Be patient and you'll eventually find the brands that you love and are happy about supporting. Your purchases from here are meant to be slow, so allow time to understand where you want to invest your money.

✳

# Write down some ethical brands you've found from your research below that you want to try!

# If in Doubt, Shop Smart

If all else fails, and you're clueless about which brands are or aren't ethical, can't find what you need, or you need affordable clothes for work, then just try your best to be smart with your money, no matter the shop you're in.

## Eco edits, conscious or recycled collections

While most big fashion brands are appalling when it comes to their responsibility surrounding human and environmental matters, there are more 'eco edits' or 'conscious collections' popping up. Hunt around to see if any brands offer collections made from more sustainable materials such as organic cotton, if they have made items from recycled materials, or whether they have supported a smaller designer. Try to buy items from these collections to show the brand that this is what the consumer wants. If more of us did this, these collections would start to make up more of the clothes they sell. Yes, lots of this is 'greenwashing', and it isn't ideal to be buying from fast-fashion retailers, but sometimes this is the best option we have.

## Classic basics over fleeting trends

Stick to classic items such as well-fitting jeans or a classic pair of heels so that the clothes you buy will actually last in your wardrobe. Try to avoid getting sucked into trends. If you're only buying it because everyone else is wearing it, stop and think twice about whether it's something that will stand the test of time.

## Brands that do it best

Find a brand that does one thing and does it well. That might be jeans, or T-shirts, or even socks. They're experts for a reason, and people love their stuff because it's good. They're likely to have more details about the materials they're using, where their clothes are made, who by, and why they're so good at what they do. Plus by focusing on a core range of designs, they're not producing as much waste or product overall.

## Make it last

Have in mind that what you're buying and only buy what you'll be wearing for years to come. This is the way we should all approach fashion in order to create sustainable wardrobes that will stand the test of time.

# four

—

# health and beauty

# Minimal Beauty

Let's all stop listening to the media about what insecurities will be solved by the latest beauty trend, and instead became confident in our natural beauty. The beauty industry profits from our insecurities, telling us our body hair is embarrassing, our wrinkles are unattractive, our hips are too big or our hair too frizzy. It makes sense for them to do this: the beauty industry is big business, with the market value for beauty and personal care hitting £13.7 billion in the UK in 2018.[22] There is no end to the beauty ideals we are taught to uphold, and it's honestly exhausting.

Learning to love your natural beauty, and appreciating yourself without makeup, can be a really difficult thing to do. I've had my fair share of moments looking in the mirror hating what I saw. A lot of that came from the insecurities I'd been conditioned to have – I was told I needed lots of foundation and concealer to cover my skin, and I should straighten my waves, shave my hairy legs, shrink my nose and use all sorts of products to make myself more 'beautiful'. I call bullshit. None of this made me happy. It only made me nervous to leave the house without makeup, develop an eating disorder and social anxiety, and become ashamed of my natural appearance. And my experience isn't unique.

We are becoming more and more insecure about our appearance, often seeking extreme measures to 'fix' our looks: getting invasive surgery, going on extreme diets and spending our money on treatments to look like the photoshopped celebrities in magazines and perfectly posed pictures on Instagram. With an increasing amount of young people using social media, it's even easier for children, teenagers and adults alike to use the Facetune app to change the look of their bodies and faces to appear nothing like they do in real life. It's scary how easily accessible such apps and filters are to everyone and anyone, potentially causing damaging effects to your own body image, and to anyone following your account. We are developing new identity issues as a result of the unrealistic beauty standards seen all over the media. Our phones are our new worlds, and we are spending more time looking at an idealised world of flat stomachs and flawless skin than at the real world, full of diversity and all body shapes and sizes.

All of this makes me, understandably, pretty mad. As someone who adored watching beauty gurus, copied fashion bloggers' outfits and wanted to be just like the girls in fashion magazines, it negatively impacted how I saw myself. When I realised I couldn't keep up with them, it made me feel like I wasn't as impressive or worthy as they were. This trend makes young impressionable people feel that they aren't enough by themselves, which is absolutely devastating. Beauty is not an indicator of your worth, nor does it only show up in the limited and unrealistic version of beauty we see in adverts and movies and all over Instagram.

This is exactly why I want you to get to know your natural skin, hair and body; to minimise your beauty routine and learn to love what you've got, without trying to change it. And in case you haven't been reminded of it lately, what you have in this very moment, how you look right now, is enough. Whatever body shape, skin tone, hair type you are – it's worthy. It's hard to let go of insecurities that have been ingrained in us, or the way we've been treated because of our appearance, but the longer you practise self-love, the easier it becomes to let go of these insecurities and embrace your natural beauty.

Small changes – such as using fewer products on your skin, regularly not wearing makeup, or just not spending so much time picking apart your appearance in the mirror – will make a startling difference to your confidence, time and bank balance. As soon as I started switching over to more natural alternatives, I no longer felt the pressure of having to wear a certain amount of makeup in order to be presentable and leave the house. I also left behind the burden of having to spend a fortune regularly restocking my makeup and beauty products. Plus, I have an awful lot more time in the mornings!

You don't *need* the latest makeup palette, you don't *need* to get plastic surgery and you don't *need* to shave your armpits. But maybe you like wearing colourful eyeshadow because it makes you feel happy or you get plastic surgery for you and nobody else. Just don't alter your appearance to meet anyone else's standards.

## Toxic beauty and beauty waste

Similar to the fashion industry, the beauty industry is shockingly wasteful. More than 120 billion units of packaging are produced every year by the global cosmetics industry, most of which isn't recyclable.[23] Just think about the amount of money you've spent in the past on beauty products that have ended up half used or in the bin. Shampoos, conditioners, moisturisers, toothpastes, shaving creams – you name it, it comes in layers of plastic packaging. That plus the toxic chemicals and animal-tested ingredients are all good reasons to think twice about your beauty purchases.

It's pretty rare to come across beauty products that don't involve any plastic packaging. But it's popping up more and more as consumers become more conscious. We are quite literally covering our planet and filling our oceans with plastic, just so we can look good. Sadly, excessive and luxurious packaging is considered more high-end or premium. This especially extends to the lavish and 'Instagrammable' PR packages that are sent out with the intention of being unboxed in front of influencers' large audiences.

One of the hardest parts of decluttering for me was throwing away so much wasted product and packaging that couldn't be recycled, or that family and friends didn't want – stuff that made me break out, made my hair greasy or my skin itch. If you were to look in your makeup bag or bathroom right now, how much of it do you honestly use on a daily or weekly basis? It can be shocking how much we actually use and need against how much we buy and keep.

When I started looking into minimising my routine and making my own beauty products I was surprised by how much you can make at home with the same, if not better, results as the things you're buying in the shops. Oils, vinegars and clays, for example, are amazing multipurpose ingredients that you can buy in bulk and use again and again for so many purposes.

There are also so many harsh chemicals in the products we are slathering all over our bodies and pouring down the drain. Parabens, parfums, SLS, triclosan, BHA, BHT, coal tar dyes, DEA, formaldehyde, heavy metals, mineral oils and petroleum are just some of the ingredients regularly found in everyday cosmetic products that have been shown to cause harm to our bodies and to the environment. Many of the ingredients in mascaras, moisturisers and sunscreens are toxic to aquatic life and coral reefs. Similarly, these chemicals can potentially irritate the skin, cause acne, premature ageing, disrupt hormones[24], or are carcinogenic.[25] This is why it's increasingly important to read labels, do your own research and understand what chemicals we should aim to avoid and find alternatives for.

# Top Tips to Reduce Your Beauty Waste:

- Buy bigger bottles that will last longer, therefore creating less waste.
- Swap bottles of hand wash or body wash for a bar of soap.
- Try out a shampoo bar instead of a bottle of shampoo.
- Use everything up, cutting packaging open to get everything out (this works well for tubes of concealer or foundation).
- Return your packaging to the brand you bought it from to send a message.
- Support eco-friendly brands using recycled plastic in their packaging, and offering package-free options or refills.
- When travelling, fill up smaller refill bottles instead of buying travel-sized toiletries.
- Buy and use less products overall and opt for multipurpose products such as hair and body soap.
- Make your own products (see later in this chapter for all the beauty recipes).

## Cruelty-free beauty

Nowadays, so much of the makeup and skincare on the shelves of department stores has sadly been tested on animals. It can be particularly hard to tell what is and isn't cruelty-free, as the term isn't regulated; any brand can claim to be so. The only way a company can be totally cruelty-free is when no animal testing has happened at *any* point during production. That means the ingredients, raw materials and the finished product can't be tested on animals by them, or any third parties. There are a lot of companies out there claiming not to test on animals, but they still sell in China where animal testing is required by law.

Alternatives to animal testing have become more viable over the last two decades, making it much harder to justify still using animals to test the safety of beauty products.[26] Thankfully in the UK and the European Union, animal testing has been banned, and fingers crossed more and more countries around the world will implement a similar ban. This is why it's important to support cruelty-free companies and boycott brands that finance animal testing.

I usually stick to companies that make it very clear that they are cruelty-free or vegan, with obvious certification and confirmation for these claims on their websites and on cruelty-free/vegan blogs. If you're still confused about whether your favourite brand is cruelty-free or not, you can email them asking about their stance on animal testing, and whether they sell in China or not. If their response is that they do sell in China, or something akin to 'we only test on animals when required by law', then they unfortunately aren't cruelty-free. Be sure to let them know that you won't be able to support them until they change their policies. Don't be fooled by their language, as they'll try to spin it in the best light possible.

Check out Cruelty-Free Kitty and Logical Harmony for a full list of brands that test on animals and are cruelty-free.

Don't forget that 'cruelty-free' and 'vegan' do not mean the same thing. There are a lot of brands nowadays using phrases such as 'vegan formula' to sell products that aren't cruelty-free – they won't contain animal ingredients, but they may well have been tested on animals, or be made by a brand that does.

Be wary of this and don't be tricked by clever marketing. Big companies are also jumping on the vegan bandwagon (or 'veganwashing', as it's become known) by creating brands that are described as 'vegan' despite being made by companies that test on animals.

If you are vegan be mindful of ingredients such as beeswax, collagen and lanolin, which are commonly found in beauty products. Get used to reading labels like you do for food, to find out what products a brand makes which are or aren't vegan. Lots of cruelty-free companies nowadays label their products 'suitable for vegans' to make the process easier for us!

Luckily, a lot of natural or sustainable beauty brands are also cruelty-free and/or vegan, making things a lot easier! And if you start to make your own products, you'll be able to minimise the volume of products you're purchasing overall, and therefore the amount of investigation needed.

# Decluttering Your Toiletries

Time to revisit our step-by-step decluttering guide before we learn more about minimal beauty. Remember to use stuff up if you can, recycle packaging, gift things to friends and throw anything out that is expired. Just as with your clothing, simply looking at how many toiletries you have accumulated can be a big reality check. Keep in mind what things you haven't used so you don't end up buying them again.

# ① CHOOSE AN AREA

## CATEGORY

MAKEUP
SKINCARE
BODY
PERFUME
HAIRCARE
FEMININE HYGIENE
MEDICINE AND SUPPLEMENTS
BEAUTY TOOLS
BABY AND CHILD

## AREA

BATHROOM CABINET/CUPBOARD
SINK
SHOWER
BATH
SHELVES
MAKEUP BAG
STORAGE BOXES
DRESSING TABLE
DRAWERS

# ② TAKE EVERYTHING OUT

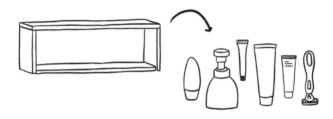

# Minimal and Natural Makeup Routine

I want to share my simple go-to minimal makeup routine. I have learnt to love my bare face as much as I love myself with makeup, which is a huge step for someone who used to find it impossible to leave the house without makeup on. Nowadays when I wear makeup I usually do a very simple, quick and easy routine that makes me feel pretty, but still like myself. Take some ideas from this routine and make it your own: it will only take five minutes of your morning and you're good to go!

1   BB CREAM/LIGHT FOUNDATION

I skip the heavy foundation and instead opt for a light-coverage BB cream or foundation for my base. I just apply it on the parts that need it, focusing on the centre. This way you can see my freckles and skin tone, but everything is evened out. I apply the cream with my fingers to save time and for a more natural application.

2   CONCEALER

Some days I skip the BB cream altogether and just use concealer. I use the product mostly under my eyes, as well as around my nose and on my chin. I layer the product up rather than applying a lot at once to make sure I end up with a light coverage.

3   MASCARA

I usually skip eyeshadow, leaving my eyelids bare with a natural eye 'shadow', and go straight to mascara. Try skipping the mascara in this routine for a 'no makeup makeup' look. My best tip for extra-long lashes is to wiggle the mascara at the root, and then brush up for a great lift.

4   CREAM BLUSHER

I absolutely love cream blusher since switching a few years ago. It's dewy, buildable and gives a really lovely, natural glow.

5 BRONZER/CONTOUR

Bronzer is a good way to bring some warmth and definition to the face around the cheekbones and the temples after applying your foundation. Use a bigger fluffy brush to make it more natural and light.

6 LIP BALM

I usually opt for lip balm, or, if I am feeling fancy, I'll use some lipstick or lipgloss. I love keeping my lips hydrated, and if I could only use one makeup product, it would be lip balm!

7 EYEBROW PENCIL

I'm lucky to have pretty bushy eyebrows thanks to being a hairy person in general, so my eyebrows don't take much work! I like to use an eyebrow pencil that also has a brush. I comb through my hairs and then lightly colour them in with gentle strokes.

## Magical natural beauty ingredients

One of the best parts about making your own products is that the ingredients are all versatile. They can be used on your skin, in your hair, to clean, to soothe cuts or skin issues, and even in your food. They're also often things you already have in your home!

### Here are my favourite multipurpose magical ingredients:

1 APPLE CIDER VINEGAR

Not only does it help to fight dandruff, condition the scalp and detangle your hair, but apple cider vinegar can be used as a toner for your skin, aiding hyper-pigmentation.

2 COCONUT OIL

One of the best multipurpose ingredients to have in your household, coconut oil is a moisturising powerhouse. It is super-hydrating and therefore perfect to apply to your legs after shaving, on your feet overnight, or as a last-minute lip balm. It can also be used on its own as a natural deodoriser!

3 AVOCADO

Avocados nourish the skin from the outside as much as they do from the inside. Use up a slightly overripe avocado in a hydrating face mask with some lemon, or use it to soothe sunburn.

4 SEA SALT

Loaded with minerals and anti-inflammatory properties, adding sea salt to your bath will soothe your muscles. Spritzing salt water on your hair using a spray bottle can give you that wavy beachy look.

5 LEMONS

If you're blonde, try using lemon juice to naturally bring out the lighter tones in your hair. Lemons are also conditioning, so work amazingly as a moisturising rinse after washing your hair.

6 SHEA BUTTER

Creamy, moisturising and anti-inflammatory, the fatty acids and vitamins in shea butter soften and soothe the skin. Use it all over your body to moisturise and hydrate.

7 ALOE VERA

Known for its healing properties, aloe is perfect for all skin types, to soothe sunburn, wounds or cuts. It is also a great natural gel for your hair and a calming treatment for dandruff or psoriasis.

8 TEA TREE OIL

Its antimicrobial properties make this multipurpose essential oil incredible at soothing acne, infections, cold sores, chickenpox, eczema, psoriasis, stings or insect bites.

9 ARGAN OIL

One of my favourite oils, argan oil works amazingly as a facial moisturiser, makeup remover, and through the ends of your hair to smooth and de-frizz.

10 COFFEE

Coffee grounds are a beautiful natural exfoliant to rub over your body that will leave you glowing and silky smooth.

# Beginner's Tips

Before I share some of my favourite recipes for your new minimal beauty regime, I wanted to recommend a few hacks to get you started!

1 RECYCLE

Save any old jam, nut butter or pickle jars to use for your homemade recipes. Also keep any nice spray bottles, containers or tubs from your toiletries when they run out.

2 STERILISE

These jars have to be totally sterilised before using them. First wash them in soapy water, and then pour over boiling hot water and leave to soak. I often repeat this process in order to remove any labels.

3 GET RESEARCHING

Hopefully I can get you started on your journey to making your own beauty products and minimising your beauty routine. However, I definitely recommend you get online and learn all about all the different ingredients that are good or bad for your own skin and hair types, and what you can make at home.

4 GATHER INGREDIENTS

Read through this chapter, decide on a few recipes you want to give a go, and start to gather your ingredients! Easy things to buy first are oils that can be multipurpose – such as coconut or argan oil, essential oils that will make everything smell lovely – or even apple cider vinegar, which can be used as much for your hair and skin as it can in a salad dressing.

5 SPOT TEST

If you have sensitive skin, it might be a good idea to test new ingredients. Simply use a small amount on your neck or on your arm to see if it reacts.

# Skin

It's our biggest organ, so taking care of our skin is very important. If you're experiencing breakouts, try to figure out if there might be a reason behind this. It could be related to stress levels, diet, water consumption, etc. Of course, seek out professional help if you're concerned.

I find that not wearing as much makeup, using natural skincare, reducing my alcohol intake, drinking lots of water, and eating a healthy and varied diet all help to keep my skin in good condition. But remember not to beat yourself up if you do experience breakouts: they're totally normal!

## Oatmeal and almond scrub

Perfect for all skin types, this scrub is gentle and anti-inflammatory due to the main ingredient: oats. It doesn't involve sugar or salt, which can be harsh on the skin on your face, so it will exfoliate while retaining moisture. Oatmeal also contains saponins, which act as a cleansing agent without stripping the skin or leaving it feeling tight. Almonds contain vitamin E, which is not only an antioxidant but helps prevent cell damage. Use once or twice a week for super soft skin.

INGREDIENTS
½ cup oats
½ cup almond meal

METHOD
1 Blend together the ingredients in a food processor until a fine mixture has been made. Store in a container.
2 Pour out around 1 tsp into the palm of your hand, and add a few splashes of water to turn it into a paste (I recommend doing this in the shower as it can get a bit messy in the sink).
3 Rub the paste gently over your face. Use more of the mixture if using on your body.
4 Wash off gently with water.

## Facial oil

Switching to oils was the best skincare decision I've ever made. Not only does it feel luxurious, but it's both gentle and moisturising. If you are acne prone or suffer with breakouts, don't be afraid to give oils a try! The reason oils work so well is that plant oils are very similar to those produced by your skin naturally, meaning that they can moisturise without clogging your pores.

**A few notes before you mix together your own concoction:**

- Avoid coconut oil as this is comedogenic and can therefore clog pores.
- Get yourself a small 1-ounce dropper bottle.
- There are many essential oils, carrier oils and nourishing oils you can use for your own facial oil, so the options are endless! I wanted to share a beginner's option, to keep it simple.
- A little goes a long way. I'm talking 3-5 drops at a time. This is where a lot of people go wrong with oils – don't overuse them!
- Make sure to always cleanse before using a facial oil.
- Use water! Trying to moisturise your face with a few drops of oil when dry will be an uncomfortable task. Use straight out of the shower, or simply dampen your face before using to help the oils glide over.

METHOD

1 Pour your chosen carrier oil around ½ to ⅔ of the way into your bottle.
2 Add in the nourishing oil until the bottle is nearly full.
3 Add in 4–7 drops of essential oil. Less is more with essential oils, as they are very potent. Begin with 4 drops, give it a shake and a sniff, and only add more if you feel it's needed. It shouldn't smell overpowering, and if your skin is sensitive, stick to less, or none at all.

TO USE

1 Pour 3–5 drops into the palm of your hand and apply to a cleansed, damp face.
2 Smooth and pat gently all over your face and neck.

## My facial oil

You might be curious to know what is in my own personal facial oil! As someone with combination skin, this mixture works perfectly for me. I added in a few drops of vitamin E oil for its nourishing properties. Lavender is one of my favourite calming smells, making my skincare routine feel like I'm at a spa.

INGREDIENTS

⅔ jojoba oil
⅓ rose hip oil
5–7 drops of lavender essential oil
3–5 drops of vitamin E oil

Simply add all of the ingredients into a small bottle with a pipette and shake together to mix.

## Oil cleanser

The idea of using oil to cleanse your skin can seem weird. I was always under the impression you needed some kind of soap to wash dirt and makeup off your skin. That was until I gave oil cleansing a go.

Oil cleansing is based on the principle of like dissolves like. Oils can actually help to remove the oils from your face, without stripping them completely away. Similar to our hair, over-stripping the natural sebum produced on our skin or scalp can encourage it to produce more. This creates that endless cycle of clogged pores, an oilier T-zone and greasy scalp.

I love oil cleansing because not only does it remove dirt and makeup, but it leaves your skin feeling moisturised, rather than tight and dry. Many swear by this method, so don't knock it until you've tried it!

To make your cleansing oil, you'll need a base of castor oil, along with a carrier oil. Popular carrier oils can include jojoba, sweet almond, grapeseed, avocado, sunflower seed, olive, organ and tamarau. See the chart on pages 138–139 to learn what benefits each of these oils have for your skin type. If you try this method and find that your skin is breaking out, do some more research and give it a go with a different carrier oil until you find what works.

This guide is a good place to start, based on your skin type. From there you can adjust according to your own unique needs.

| OILY | NORMAL | DRY |
|---|---|---|
| ⅓ carrier oil | ½ carrier oil | ⅔ carrier oil |
| ⅔ castor oil | ½ castor oil | ⅓ castor oil |

METHOD

1  Pour around a teaspoon of oil into the palms of clean hands and rub all over your skin. If wearing makeup, start with the skin, then gently rub over your lashes and eyelids. You will look like a panda, but at least the makeup is coming off!

2  Rinse hands and run a clean facecloth under a hot tap. My favourite cloth to use is bamboo, as I find it the softest and most effective; however, any flannel will work fine.

3  If you're wearing makeup, gently remove using the facecloth in circular motions, and then you can either stop there, or continue by following the next step to cleanse your skin without any makeup.

4  When the facecloth is nice and hot, wring it out and place over your face. You can lean back and let this sit over your face until it has cooled down.

5  Once cooled, use the facecloth to rub the oil into your skin in circular motions, starting from the bottom upwards (be sure not to rub too hard).

6  After oil cleansing, it's optional to use moisturiser. I usually follow with my facial oil in the evenings. The great thing about oil cleansing is that you don't necessarily need to moisturise afterwards.

## CARRIER/BASE OILS

**Argan oil** (all skin types)

**Sweet almondy oil** (dry/ageing skin/acne)

**Jojoba oil** (all skin types/acne)

**Avocado oil** (dry/ageing skin)

**Hemp seed oil** (all skin types)

**Grapeseed oil** (normal/oily/acne)

**Apricot kernal oil** (dry/ageing)

## NOURISHING OILS (OPTIONAL)

**Tamanu oil** (oily/acne/scarred/skin problems)

**Borage oil** (all skin types/oily/acne/eczyma)

**Emu oil** (dry/ageing)

**Sea buckthorn oil** (all skin types/ageing/dry)

**Evening primrose oil** (all skin stypes/ageing/dry)

## ESSENTIAL OIL

**Lavender oil** (oily/acne/normal/dry)

**Lemongrass oil** (dry/ageing skin/acne)

**Peppermint oil** (acne/oily)

**Chamomile oil** (all skin types)

**Ylang ylang oil** (acne/oily/ageing skin)

**Geranium oil** (ageing/dry/normal/sensitive)

**Palmarosa oil** (all skin types/ageing/breakouts)

**Rosemary oil** (acne/oily)

**Frankincense oil** (all skin types/ageing)

| | Non-greasy | Lightweight | Anti-inflammatory | Anti-ageing | Antioxidants | Antibacterial | Antiseptic | Protective | Strengthening | Blood circulation | Astringent | Calming | Healing | Nourishing | Rejuvenating | Firming | Hydrating | Regulates oil | Softening |
|---|---|---|---|---|---|---|---|---|---|---|---|---|---|---|---|---|---|---|---|
| | ✹ | | | ✹ | | | | | | | | | ✹ | | | | ✹ | | |
| | | | | | | | | | | | | | ✹ | ✹ | | | ✹ | | |
| | ✹ | ✹ | | | | ✹ | | | | | | | | | | | | | |
| | | | | ✹ | | | | | | | | | ✹ | | | | ✹ | | ✹ |
| | | ✹ | | ✹ | | | | ✹ | | | | | | | | | | | |
| | | ✹ | | | ✹ | | | | | | | | | | | | | ✹ | |
| | | ✹ | ✹ | | | ✹ | | | | | | | | | | | ✹ | | |
| | | | | | | | | | | | | | ✹ | | ✹ | | | | |
| | | | ✹ | | | | | | | | | | | | | | | | |
| | | | | ✹ | | | | ✹ | | | | | | | | | | | |
| | | | | | | | | | | | | | ✹ | | ✹ | | | | |
| | | | | | | | | | | | ✹ | | | | | | ✹ | | |
| | | | | | | ✹ | ✹ | | | | | | | | | | | | |
| | | | | | | | ✹ | | ✹ | | ✹ | | | | | | | | |
| | | | | | | | | | | | | ✹ | | | | | | | |
| | | | | | | | | | | | | ✹ | ✹ | | | | | | |
| | | | | ✹ | | | | | | | | | | | | | ✹ | ✹ | |
| | | | | | | | | | | | | | | | | | | ✹ | |
| | | | | | | | | | | | | ✹ | | | | | | | ✹ |
| | | | | ✹ | | | ✹ | ✹ | | | | | | | ✹ | ✹ | | | |
| | | | | ✹ | | | | | | | | | | | ✹ | | | | |

139

## Facial mist

This works as a toner in between a cleansing and facial oil. I also love spritzing it on my face when I need a bit of a refresh, or after I've applied makeup to give myself a glow. I use a recycled spray bottle that I cleaned out to save buying a new one!

INGREDIENTS

1 tea bag *(peppermint, green or chamomile tea)*
2–3 drops of lavender essential oil

METHOD

1 Steep the tea bag in boiling water and leave to cool.
2 Add the tea and essential oil to a spray bottle, shake and spray when needed!

*Top tip!*
Try adding aloe vera for a cooling effect, or a few drops of jojoba oil for extra hydration.

## Lip scrub

Lip scrubs are a really easy product to make at home. They taste yummy and leave your lips feeling plump and soft.

INGREDIENTS

2 tbsp jojoba oil
1 tbsp caster sugar
3–5 drops of peppermint essential oil

METHOD

1 Combine all ingredients and store in a small clean jar or dish.
2 Apply a small amount to your lips and gently scrub with your finger.
3 Wash off with water and enjoy your silky smooth lips!

# Lip balm

I am totally addicted to lip balms, as I love my lips to feel soft. This homemade version is buttery soft and smells good enough to eat!

INGREDIENTS

    1 tbsp shea butter
    ½ tbsp coconut oil
    1 tsp vanilla extract

METHOD

1 Melt the shea butter and coconut oil together in a pan over a low heat.
2 Stir in the vanilla.
3 Pour into a container and allow to set in the fridge. I always clean out an old small jar that I have either from an old lip balm or moisturiser for this.
4 Store in a cool dry place. If you live in a hot country, store in the fridge.

*Top tip!*

    For a lip plump, add in a pinch of cinnamon.
    For a lip stain, add in 1 tbsp of raspberry powder.

## Skin type

Before making your own DIY creations for your face, you need
to understand your skin type. This will allow you to pick the
right ingredients to complement your skin. Follow the simple
chart below to discover exactly what your skin type is.

| OILY | NORMAL |
|---|---|
| Enlarged pores<br>Shiny all over<br>Acne and blackhead prone | Pores barely visible<br>Even texture and tone<br>Neither dry nor oily<br>Relatively blemish free |
| **COMBINATION** | **DRY** |
| Medium pores<br>Shiny on T-zone and chin<br>Dry/normal on rest of the face<br>Prone to blackheads | Invisible pores<br>Scaly and flaky<br>Prone to red patches |
| **AGEING OR SUN-DAMAGED** | **SENSITIVE** |
| Fine lines and wrinkles<br>Hyperpigmentation<br>Loose skin due to loss of elasticity | Delicate and fine pores<br>Red patches and irritation<br>Broken capillaries around<br>the nose and cheeks<br>Easily irritated by new products |

# Hair

The main issue when caring for our hair is the frequency with which we wash it, use heat and mess with it. The ingredients found in lots of commercial haircare brands strip it of its natural oils (sebum) leaving it greasy after a day or two. The amount of heat we use every day to style it changes the natural shape of our hair, as well as creating split ends. Bleach and hair dye can very often leave our hair lifeless and damaged.

## Hair type

Just like our skin, we all have varying hair types. Understanding our hair type will really help us to discover how to better look after it, and how much our hair can handle. All hair types can benefit from simplifying hair products and routines to allow our hair to do its thing.

| | A | B | C |
|---|---|---|---|
| 1 | Pin straight<br>Fine<br>Thin<br>Soft<br>Difficult to style | Straight with<br>bend at ends<br>Medium texture<br>Most common<br>straight hair | Slight bends<br>Slightly coarser<br>Thick<br>Can be frizzy<br>Common among<br>Asian women |
| 2 | S-pattern beachy waves<br>Fine<br>Thin<br>Lacks volume<br>and definition | Defined waves<br>Medium texture<br>Can be frizzy | Tight waves with<br>some curls<br>Coarse<br>Thick<br>Frizzy |
| 3 | Springy and loose<br>S-pattern defined curls<br>Volume | Stretched springy curls<br>Smaller curls<br>Very voluminous<br>Slightly coarser<br>Frizzy | Corkscrew curls<br>Textured<br>Coarse<br>Frizzy<br>Dense |
| 4 | Tight, springy coils<br>Falls down<br>Fine and wiry<br>Dense | Z crimpy kinks<br>Clearly defined at ends<br>High density | Z-shaped<br>No defined curl pattern<br>Variety of textures<br>Over 75% shrinkage |

## What to avoid/reduce

### SILICONES

Silicones are basically a rubber or plastic barrier that sticks to the hair to make it smooth and shiny. It's used in most haircare products because it gives the illusion of healthy hair. However, silicones can build up on your hair over time, leaving it waxy, limp and lifeless. As they are a sealant, they will prevent moisture from penetrating your hair shaft and dirt will easily stick to it. Particularly if you have curly hair, silicones can be problematic, as the shape and texture of your hair leaves it prone to more buildup. There are many different names for silicones (look out for words ending in 'cone'), but try to find brands that explicitly say 'silicone-free' on their packaging; or simply contact the manufacturers to find out more.

### SULFATES

Sulfates cleanse your hair. They're what makes your shampoo bubble in the shower. Sulfates are used in products such as toothpaste, face wash and shower gels to make them lather and therefore easier to scrub away dirt. While they do well at removing the grime, dead skin cells and dirt, they can also take away the natural oils along with it. For some, this can leave your hair dry and brittle, or even irritate your scalp, causing itching and dryness. Your scalp will try to replace these oils, making your hair greasy, faster, and your dry hair frizzier. The three most common sulfates you'll see in your products are SLS (sodium laurel sulfate) or ALS (ammonium laureth sulfate).

### PARABENS

Parabens are a preservative more typically found in skincare, but they still make their way into hair products. They stop bacteria or fungus from growing in your products that are often kept in moist places such as the bathroom. Parabens contain xenoestrogen, which means they can mimic oestrogen in our bodies as they are easily absorbed through the skin. Parabens are also bad for the environment, as they have been found in the bodies of marine mammals. There are now many alternatives, which means parabens aren't necessary in our day-to-day lives.

### OVER-WASHING

Over-washing hair will teach it to replenish the oils you've stripped away, making your hair greasier, faster. Stretch out the days from every day to every other day. Then from every other day to every three days. Wear your hair up in a bun on those greasy hair days! Over time you'll train your hair to stop needing to be washed so regularly. This will also be helped if you avoid the ingredients I've mentioned above. Look forward to the prospect of only having to wash your hair once or twice a week!

### HEAT

It's no surprise that heat damages hair. It removes the moisture, making it dehydrated and dry. Your hair becomes more rigid and brittle when you overuse heat, allowing it to break off more easily, causing split ends and hair that won't grow. Allowing your hair to dry naturally will let it return to its natural shape, maintain moisture and experience fewer breakages. Try weaning yourself off by only using heat on special occasions, switching to the cool setting on your hair dryer, or only partially drying your hair with a hairdryer.

### BLEACH

It should go without saying, but bleach and other harsh hair dyes are extremely damaging to your hair. They change its porosity, strip it of its moisture, and often lead to more brittle hair over time. While it's fun to experiment with hair colours, if you have a hair type that is easily damaged, and is clearly suffering from all the different colours you're dyeing it, give it a break!

## No poo

Firstly, what on earth is no poo? Don't worry – it doesn't mean to not poo! It's a shortened phrase meaning 'no shampoo' (I'm a little mad at the person who came up with the term), while also eliminating commercial products from your routine, avoiding in particular silicones, sulfates and parabens. It can be a hard process, especially if you have used normal shampoos and conditioners on your hair your whole life. However, given time, it can work wonders for lots of people and their hair!

## No-poo methods

WATER ONLY

Water only is the ultimate minimalist haircare routine. It's as simple as saying goodbye to all products and only using water. I gave this a go and it did surprisingly well to train my hair not to become so greasy so fast, but I did miss that 'just-washed' feeling. The idea is that the natural oils on your scalp will condition, protect and nourish your hair. Having hard water or an oilier hair type may prevent this method from working for you. But for some it can be a great natural alternative!

### Find out your water type!

- Search your location online or contact your water provider.
- If you notice a lot of limescale in your sink/kettle and on your cutlery, then you have hard water.
- If you live in a city, you probably have hard water. If you live remotely, you probably have soft water.

METHOD

1  Leave your hair to get oily before washing. The longer you wait, the better your hair will get at regulating its natural oil production.

2  Scritch, preen and brush! You can do this every day, or the night before washing with water. Scritching (another charming word) involves rubbing your scalp with your fingertips, similar to how you would when washing your hair in the shower. This will help to loosen the oils and skin on your scalp. It will also increase blood flow which can encourage hair growth! Preening involves pinching small sections of your hair between two fingers and sliding them down the length of your hair in order to distribute

the oils evenly. Finally, brushing with a wooden brush will detangle and further distribute the oils throughout the hair. As your hair gets used to regulating the oil on your scalp, you can skip the scritching and preening, and just stick to brushing.

3 Wash! Wet hair under warm or hot water and rub your scalp, just without the shampoo! If you have long or thick hair, try sectioning it off to really get in there. Over time it will become less hard work.

4 Rinse with cold water to retain moisture and leave your hair looking shiny.

## ACID ONLY

Using an acid rinse to wash your hair, such as diluted apple cider vinegar, distilled white vinegar or lemon juice, is another no poo method that helps to distribute oils while conditioning your hair. While the term 'acid' sounds scary, these 'acids' all sit at a similar pH level to your scalp. This is great if you've given 'water only' a go and find it too drying, that your hair is still oily, or there is waxy buildup. An acidic rinse can also be used alongside a normal shampoo and conditioning routine to moisturise the scalp and leave your hair feeling nourished and shiny.

## Acidic rinses

**Apple cider vinegar** – highly moisturising – dry hair, dry scalp

**Distilled white vinegar** – lightly moisturising – oily scalp

### METHOD

1 Mix a couple of tablespoons of vinegar into a jar or container with water (add more vinegar as needed – test the results and adjust).

2 Once your hair is wet, pour the rinse over your head and scrub in as you would shampoo and rinse out with water. If you have hard water, do this on dry hair, and then rinse it out with water. The rinse can also be left in for those with coarse or dry hair.

## pH-balanced wash methods

Soapnuts, shikakai, chickpea/gram flour, rye flour and oat milk all have the same pH level as our scalp. They therefore work amazingly by themselves to cleanse the hair.

---

## Tea rinse

This is one of my favourite natural ways to wash my hair. It leaves it feeling soft, clean and conditioned. It can be a messy method, but as I wash my hair so much less now, this is fine by me. 'Oiling' your hair before doing a tea rinse is a great option for those with coarse and curly hair types, to nourish the hair. An acid rinse can also be used following the tea, to condition.

As it takes a bit of preparation, this doesn't need to be something you do every time you wash your hair, but can be a nourishing treat for your hair when you fancy a pamper.

The powders I'm using for this tea rinse are shikakai, neem and amla. Shikakai will cleanse the hair, neem is great for dandruff or a dry scalp, and amla will moisturise and condition.

INGREDIENTS

    1 tbsp shikakai powder
    ½ tbsp neem powder
    ½ tbsp amla powder

METHOD

1 Boil 2 cups of water in the kettle or on the stove.
2 Add the powders to the water and boil for a minute or until a foam forms.
3 Take off the heat and leave to steep overnight.
4 The following day, pour the tea through a sieve to remove any gritty bits.
5 Pour into a squeeze bottle or an applicator for your hair (using an old shampoo bottle would work fine).
6 Wet hair and apply the tea rinse all over your head. Use the bottle to apply it to all areas of your scalp.
7 Scrub and massage the scalp gently, leave for 30 seconds, and then rinse thoroughly.

## Alkaline wash methods

Bicarbonate of soda, clay washes and quinoa can be used to wash the hair alongside a follow-up acid rinse to balance the pH of the scalp.

## Clay detox

The best clays to opt for are bentonite or rhassoul clay. They can be used alone with water, followed by an acid rinse, or you can give the recipe below a go!

INGREDIENTS

    1 cup water
    ⅓ cup apple cider vinegar
    ⅔ cup clay
    10 drops of essential oil *(optional)*

METHOD

1   Pour the water and apple cider vinegar into a non-metal bowl and stir.
2   Add a tablespoon of clay at a time, whisking together as you add it in.
3   Keep adding clay until you create a yoghurt/egg-like texture.
4   Add in your essential oils if using.
5   To use, massage a handful into wet hair, rubbing into the roots and coating the hair. Leave for 5–10 minutes (don't let dry!), and rinse out with warm water.
6   You can store this in an airtight container for up to a week.

## OH poo

OH stands for hydroxide, a key part of saponification, where fats or oils are made into soap, e.g. Castile soap, shampoo bars and African black soap. These are an easy option to go for when minimising your haircare routine, that can be complemented by an acid rinse for conditioning. These will save on a lot of waste, last a long time and take zero effort. Nowadays I use shampoo bars the most to wash my hair!

## Low poo

Opting for commercial shampoos and conditioners that are free from parabens, silicones and sulfates is often the easiest way to approach the 'no poo' idea and is referred to as 'low poo'. If you have hard water, or want the convenience of buying a shampoo and conditioner to use rather than making your own, this is the perfect option. There are loads of brands out there now that are committing to natural products that are good for your hair.

## Conditioner only

Using only conditioner to wash your hair keeps the hair moisturised, and is often used by those following the 'curly girl' method.

## Hair refresh spray

Day two, three, four or five hair often needs a refresh. Instead of washing it when it isn't looking greasy yet, use a homemade hair spray. This is especially great for my wavy and curly girls out there.

INGREDIENTS

Aloe vera gel
Essential oils
Argan oil
Water

METHOD

1   Using an old spray bottle, add in about a tenth of the bottle with aloe vera gel, around 4–6 drops of essential oil and a few drops of argan oil. Use less or more argan oil depending on your hair type – go for less if you're worried, but my hair soaks it up!
2   Top up with water and shake it up.
3   Spritz the hair all over, give it a scrunch, and your hair should look and feel refreshed!

## Dry shampoo

This easy dry shampoo recipe will soak up the oils from your scalp if you're in the transitional stage of trying to stop washing your hair as often.

INGREDIENTS

2 tbsp arrowroot powder

2 tbsp cocoa powder *(if your hair is super light in colour, leave this out and stick to the arrowroot)*

METHOD

1   Mix ingredients together.
2   Apply to hair with a makeup brush and rub in.

# Body

Now we've covered skin and hair, it's time to explore the rest of the body! It's all about simplicity and avoiding the overuse of soaps, moisturisers and gimmicky products. If you stick to the basics, your body will thank you for it!

## Natural soaps

Finding soaps from a local shop that are made from few and natural ingredients is a great waste-free way to wash yourself. It's important not to overuse soap, or overwash with harsh chemicals and strong shower gels every single day. Like the skin on your face and scalp, overusing soaps on your body can create an imbalance in our sebum production and remove healthy bacteria. Avoid harsh soaps that contain the words 'antibacterial' on the label. Your best bet is to go for a solid soap bar, over one in a bottle with a pump.

## Moisturiser

A multipurpose moisturiser is a great start to making something homemade for your body. It's perfect for after you've shaved your legs, as a hand cream, or even as a balm for your lips. It also smells like chocolate!

INGREDIENTS

¼ cup coconut oil
½ cup shea butter
1 tsp vitamin E oil *(optional)*
6–8 drops of essential oils

METHOD

1   Melt the coconut oil in a pan over low heat *(optional)*.
2   Blend all the ingredients in a blender or food processor. Or if you don't own one, mix it together thoroughly in a bowl.
3   Decant into a recycled jar and store in cool, dry place.

# Body scrub

There is nothing better than a good old pamper with a body scrub at the weekends. It'll leave you feeling beautifully silky soft. Plus, it smells good enough to eat!

INGREDIENTS

½ cup coconut oil
¼–½ cup granulated sugar
½ tsp vanilla extract or 1 tbsp lemon, lime or orange juice *(optional)*

METHOD

1   Combine all ingredients in a bowl and mix until a smooth paste has formed. Make sure to do this with hard coconut oil as otherwise the sugar will dissolve! If you live in a hot country, put the coconut oil in the fridge beforehand to harden up.
2   Apply to the skin in a circular motion, massaging in particular into the legs, feet and arms.
3   Rinse with water, and pat dry with a towel, and prepare to feel like a newborn baby.

*Top tip!*

Be careful if using this scrub in a shower. Make sure to use the scrub at the end of your shower and clean thoroughly afterwards to avoid any slippery accidents from the coconut oil! To be super safe, rub most of the scrub off with a flannel before rinsing.

## Deodorant

Avoiding antiperspirant deodorants that contain aluminium is really important. Not only do they clog your pores in order to block the sweat glands, but the aluminium compounds are absorbed into the skin causing changes in oestrogen receptors in breast cells. It can take time to adjust to a natural deodorant – it was also odd for me to get used to the sensation of feeling sweat. But sweat is there for a reason, to cool us down! What works best for me is a salt/crystal deodorant or deodorant balms. Try out different natural alternatives until you find the one that works for you and always use natural deodorants on clean underarms to get best results.

Alternatively, you can make your own homemade concoction!

INGREDIENTS
    3 tbsp coconut oil
    2 tbsp shea butter
    2 tbsp bicarbonate of soda
    2 tbsp arrowroot powder or cornflour
    Essential oils

METHOD
1  Melt the coconut oil and shea butter together in a pan.
2  Remove from the pan and mix in the bicarbonate of soda and arrowroot/cornflour.
3  Add 5–10 drops of essential oils, just enough to create a slight scent.
4  Pour into a container and leave to cool. Something wide and flat would be the best option.
5  Use your fingers to melt a small amount on your fingertips and rub onto your underarm until it disappears.

*Top tip!*
    If you don't have shea butter, just skip this and replace the same amount with more coconut oil. Also, test using bicarbonate of soda on your skin before going ahead with this recipe, as for sensitive skin types it can be irritating.

## Body hair

As someone who rocks a dark thick head of hair, I also have a lot of body hair. I've been told my whole life by mean kids at school and the media that this is something to be heavily ashamed of. But we don't need to be ashamed of our body hair! It's natural and it's normal. *But* if you still choose to shave it off like I do, try to give yourself breaks between shaving. Not only will this let your skin recover and avoid ingrown hairs/rashes, but it'll also teach you to feel more comfortable when you *do* have hair on your body.

Coconut oil and aloe vera work wonders as shaving gel (just be careful not to slip with coconut oil in your shower – use a flannel to wipe off most of the residue). Make sure to exfoliate before shaving to avoid any irritation and get the most out of your hair removal.

I do, however, let my eyebrows pretty much do their own thing. Most of us have gone through times of over-plucking, particularly when we were younger. My best advice is to just let them be. Embrace the fact that big eyebrows are in, and give them time to regrow and frame your beautiful face.

## Periods

If you have a period, then I feel your pain. Every month. Literally. Beyond the pain, periods are also messy, expensive and pretty wasteful. The average person who has a period uses close to 10,000 tampons in their lifetime.[27] Disposable menstrual products are often flushed down the loo and the plastic wrappers end up in landfill.

Tampons and pads also contain many harsh chemicals and fibres such as surfactants, additives, adhesives, bleach, dioxin and rayon. These substances are both polluting to our bodies and to the environment.

Switching to a reusable option is a great way to lower the waste you're producing, while taking care of your body.

## MENSTRUAL CUPS

One of the most common ways nowadays to make your period more eco is a menstrual cup. This is the option I personally use, and I will never look back. It's essentially a silicone cup that you fold and insert when you're menstruating. It collects the blood throughout the day, and then you simply empty it and rinse it in a sink. Once I got the hang of it, I personally found it so much easier than tampons, as I wasn't having to change something every time I went to the loo.

It simplifies your period, making it a whole lot easier to tolerate. In between periods all you need to do is sterilise and clean your cup in some boiling water (I'll also throw in some bicarbonate of soda and lemon to remove dirt and stains). It can take time to learn how to use it, to avoid leaking and find it comfortable, but with practice, it has become a game changer for me.

Plus, as a one-off purchase, it's far more affordable than tampons. Say goodbye to late-night emergency tampon runs!

## PERIOD UNDERWEAR

If a menstrual cup doesn't take your fancy, then there are many companies nowadays coming out with period pants! They involve a padded lining that will soak up any blood during your period. It seems crazy, but it actually works. It's basically a built-in sanitary towel that is far more effective and a lot less uncomfortable. They're super comfy and appealing for those days when you just want to curl up in a ball from the pain.

## REUSABLE SANITARY PADS

Whether you make your own, or buy some online, reusable pads are another wonderful way of reducing the waste you're producing from your period. It's the same principle as a sanitary towel, except instead of throwing it away, you wash it! Think of it similarly to how you can use reusable nappies rather than disposable ones for babies.

## ORGANIC COTTON TAMPONS +
## REUSABLE TAMPON APPLICATOR

Switch to an organic cotton tampon free from chemicals, dyes and rayon that can also biodegrade (and you can throw in the compost). If you prefer using an applicator get a reusable one. You just need to give it a wipe/rinse between uses, and sterilise between periods.

Taking care of yourself and enjoying beauty isn't a bad thing. It can be a great thing! But there is a slippery slope between having fun and hiding insecurities. Use it as a form of self-care and self-expression to boost your confidence and make you feel your best. Try not to get roped into advertising campaigns that make you feel like you're missing something or need something extra to make you more beautiful. You don't! Similarly, there is a slippery slope between buying what you need and becoming a wasteful consumer. Question what you do and don't need and take control of your decisions when you're buying new products. When you start to make your own concoctions, embrace your natural beauty, become mindful of the brands you buy from, and minimise your overall routine, you'll hopefully start to see a change in how you feel about yourself. And most of all, have fun with it and remember that nobody is perfect. It's our individual quirks that make us beautiful.

# five

—

# food and drink

# Your Food Footprint

There are many ways we can all do better to reduce our carbon footprint, and how we eat is one of the biggest. If we learn about the journey our food took to get to our plate, the resources it used, the waste and ethics involved and the impact it has on the welfare of animals, the planet and the people living on it, we can try to make more informed choices. I'm not the food police, and am very mindful of how inextricably linked food, culture, mental and physical health are, but I want to share this information with you so that you can consider how small and big changes can lead you towards a more sustainable and ethical way of eating. Any changes will take time and consideration.

One of the main things we can consider reducing or eliminating altogether is animal products. A vegetarian's carbon footprint is about two-thirds of the average meat-eater's, and almost half of a meat-lover's. A vegan's is even lower.[28] In fact, eating just one less burger a week equals taking your car off the road for 320 miles.[29]

**'A global switch to diets that rely less on meat and more on fruit and vegetables could save up to 8 million lives by 2050, reduce greenhouse gas emissions by two-thirds, and lead to healthcare-related savings and avoid climate damage of $1.5 trillion (US)'** [30]

This was the conclusion of researchers at Oxford Martin School. Researchers from Oxford University assessed almost 40,000 food products across the world and concluded that 'a vegan diet is probably the single biggest way to reduce your impact on planet Earth'.[31] Not to mention that eating larger quantities of beef and processed meats has been linked to higher rates of health problems like heart disease, cancer and obesity.

The impact animal agriculture is having on our planet is shocking, and it's hard to fully quantify its environmental impact. In fact, the figures on its impact are heavily disputed. Globally we need to reduce our growing consumption of animal products but this isn't as simple as telling everyone to go vegan or vegetarian. Millions of people rely on animal products for protein, and these people, often in Indigenous communities, are not causing the problem.

What *is* causing the problem is intensive farming of animals and overconsumption of animal products. Livestock farming is one of the leading contributors to greenhouse gas emissions globally, emitting between 14.5 per cent and 18 per cent of greenhouse gasses alone.[32] One of the main ways animal agriculture contributes to global warming is through deforestation, particularly through land used to grow feed crops. Cattle ranching is said to be the 'largest driver of deforestation in every Amazon country, accounting for 80 per cent of current deforestation rates'.[33] The livestock sector is also a huge contributor to our global $CO2$ and human-caused methane emissions. Animal agriculture is the leading cause of species extinction, ocean dead zones, water pollution and habitat destruction, and its impact is only set to rise.[34] If we continue eating fish at the rate we are today, it's said that we could see fish-less oceans by 2048.[35]

We can therefore see the considerable difference between various food groups and their environmental impact, with animal products producing significantly higher emissions than plants.[36] But even different animal products have varying impacts – lamb, beef and cheese have the highest emissions. This is mainly because they come from ruminant animals that produce methane, which is 25 times more potent in its effect on the environment than carbon dioxide. It is also due to the energy-intensive food they consume, and the high amounts of manure produced by cows and sheep, compared to pigs or chickens.[37]

BEEF COMPARED TO PORK OR CHICKEN

**28 times**
more land

**6 times**
more fertiliser

**11 times**
more water

releasing
**4-5 times**
the amount of greenhouse gases [38]

<table>
<tr><td>**100g of beef**<br>= 105kg of greenhouse gases</td><td>**1lb of beef**<br>= 1,800–2,500 gallons of water</td></tr>
<tr><td>**100g of tofu**<br>= Less than 3.5kg of greenhouse gases[39]</td><td>**1lb of soy**<br>= 220 gallons of water[40]</td></tr>
</table>

Interestingly, most of the emissions created from meat occur during production, which requires vast quantities of fertiliser, pesticides, fuel, water and land. Comparatively, most of the emissions from plants are produced once the crops have left the farm – from their processing, transportation, cooking and waste disposal. Beyond greenhouse gas emissions, the billions of animals we eat produce a whole heap of manure and wastewater. This pollutes groundwater, rivers, streams and the ocean.[41]

Palm oil production is another hugely damaging industry and is one of the leading contributors to deforestation, habitat degradation, climate change, animal cruelty and Indigenous rights abuses in the countries where it takes place. The draining and burning of wetlands to make room for plant oil plantations in Indonesia shockingly accounted in 2007 for 8 per cent of all worldwide annual emissions from burning fossil fuels.[42]

As a result of climate change and industrial farming, farmers are experiencing lower yields and less nutritious foods from their harvests. Those across the world who are poverty-stricken and hungry are living in climate-stressed regions, and yet in the UK we rely on them for much of our food, as we now import over half of the food we eat.[43] As the climate continues to change, small-scale farmers will need to migrate to find food as their farms fail, making it ever more pressing for us to help combat the effects of climate change to conserve resources.

Eating seasonally and locally is another thing we can do to reduce our carbon footprint. Many of us now have access to a variety of foods all year around, whether they're in season or not, inevitably taking its toll on the environment. If we swap these for some of the foods that we can get locally, we can support farmers who are likely to be more sustainable and diverse in their farming practices, we can see where our food has come from and keep our money in the local economy.

A change towards net zero carbon emissions needs to happen so that the world can feed itself now and in the future. We need to research and support a new eco-food system that protects the natural environment, reduces greenhouse gases and supports biodiversity, all the while moving towards a more plant-based diet worldwide.[44] As individuals we can do our bit by eating more plants and less meat, buying locally and seasonally, and encouraging our local MPs, governments and companies we buy from to support sustainable farming practices and make big changes to reduce our impact.

# The Ethics of Food

## Animals

Beyond the environment, we must consider the animals and people that inhabit our planet, and how our food systems affect them. Roughly 60 billion land animals and over a trillion marine animals are used and killed as commodities per year.[45] Intensive factory farming has taken over the animal agriculture industry. If we take birds as an example, in 2016 almost a billion birds were farmed for food in Britain, 95 per cent indoors and only 3.4 per cent free-range and 1 per cent organic.[46] The welfare of animals matters greatly, and it's vital we stop treating them as less important than people, profit and the environment.

The intensity of the food system in place today inevitably affects how animals are treated, as getting as much 'product' for as low a price as possible becomes the priority. Domesticated animals have become voiceless victims within an industrial production line. We use animals for food, clothing, decoration, products, transport and our amusement, at the expense of their basic needs and happiness. Animals, like humans, experience physical and mental pain, as much as they can feel contentment and pleasure. Think of dogs, cats and other animals we keep as pets: they have unique personalities, express wants, needs and feelings – no different to cows, chickens and pigs.

If we take cows as an example, they are social animals that, in the wild, communicate and cooperate in order to survive. Like puppies or kittens, they love to play as a part of their social interaction.[47] Farmed beef cattle on average only live to 18 months old, while female calves are taken away from their mothers, put into small cages, fattened up and artificially inseminated to continue the same cycle as their mothers. Their milk can then be sold at a profit. Dairy cows will only live until the age of 4–6 years on average, despite their natural life span of up to 15–20 years. This removal of an animal's basic needs, such as the need to be with their mother, is just one example of the unethical practices that are deep-rooted in our system. It has become human interest to treat animals like machines rather than sentient beings.

Pigs are smarter than dogs and three-year-old children, yet the majority of pigs spend most of their lives in crates too small for them to even turn around.[48] Chickens are potentially the most abused on the planet, due to the scale at which we breed and slaughter them compared to all other animals. Fish are often overlooked, and yet they also feel pain.[49] They are captured and left to suffocate aboard ships after being caught in nets, which often capture other marine life such as dolphins and sharks. Between 1 and 2.7 trillion fish are annually caught globally. That's at least 150 fish per person on this planet.[50]

## Humans

When considering food ethics, we must also think of humans and whether our collective greed for a certain food puts marginalised groups in inhumane and unethical working environments. Even plant-based foods aren't free from unethical supply chains. For example, many workers in the cashew industry, earning as little as £1.70 to £2.15 a day, suffer with debilitating burns to their hands as they aren't provided with gloves to protect them from the harmful liquid that comes out of cashews.[51] Our obsession with avocado toast also comes at a cost. Much of the production of the fruit in Mexico is controlled by drug cartels, where farmers are forced to give up a percentage of their income, risking their lives if they don't.[52]

Overfishing, pollution of our waters, ocean acidification, coral bleaching and oceanwide migration of fish due to climate change are all greatly affecting communities around the world who rely on seafood as a main source of food. Indigenous people in the Arctic depend on hunting to support their local economy, and as a part of their cultural and social identity.

They consume larger amounts of fish and marine mammals and are therefore at a higher risk of exposure to pollutants.[53] Not only this, but the availability of these traditional food sources, alongside decreased safety in the changing ice and weather conditions, poses a threat to their health and food security.[54]

## Waste

Another huge issue is food waste, with around a third of all food lost or wasted along the supply chain in transport, processing or in our homes.[55] Meanwhile, 815 million of the 7.6 billion humans on the planet are severely undernourished and hungry.[56] These statistics are only set to rise as population and wealth rises. The surplus and uneven distribution of food across the world is on a scale we've never experienced before, and is largely due to our food system. We throw away imperfect-looking fruits and vegetables, eat out at restaurants who dispose of everything left on the plate, purchase a wider variety of food than ever before, and chuck away food we've forgotten to eat.

We therefore need radical change in our food systems, as well as more transparency from food suppliers about where all of their food is coming from, so that we as consumers can make more informed choices.

These statistics are scary, overwhelming and shocking. And I fear I haven't even touched the surface. The issues with our food system – where it comes from, and at what cost – is impossible to measure. It's also impossible for any of us to completely avoid, but we can do our bit to reduce. After all, learning this information is why I changed how I eat. For some of you that change may be going vegan, for others that's doing Meatless Mondays.

If everyone reduced their consumption of meat, dairy and eggs; tried to work towards a more plant-based diet overall; sought out fairtrade products; were conscious of food waste; and/or ate more locally and seasonally, we could collectively make a significant difference. So find a place where you *can* make a difference, and start today.

# What is Veganism?

**'Veganism is a way of living which seeks to exclude, as far as is possible and practicable, all forms of exploitation of, and cruelty to, animals for food, clothing or any other purpose.' – The Vegan Society [57]**

Fundamentally veganism is a plant-based diet, avoiding all meat, fish, dairy, eggs (and honey). Another element of veganism is avoiding the use of animal-derived products such as leather, wool, silk or fur, or products tested on animals, as well as choosing not to visit places where animals are kept in captivity or used for entertainment, such as the zoo, the races, or a circus that uses animals.

Veganism is on the rise, and it's a trend I'm all for. We've learnt about how much of a difference leaving animal products off your plate can be, so I want to share my best tips on how to go vegan, if you want to give it a try! Many of these tips can also be useful if you just want to reduce your overall consumption of meat and dairy.

## My top vegan tips for beginners:

1 DO IT YOUR OWN WAY

I basically went vegan overnight (though I definitely slipped up many times during those first few months), while my boyfriend took a few years of slowly reducing. We all work so differently! Changing your diet can become overwhelming if you don't allow yourself to make mistakes, or give yourself the time to plan and get used to these changes in your lifestyle. You're more likely to keep it up if you do it in your own way, at your own pace. And for you that might mean being 'plant-based' or 'flexitarian' (or ditch the labels altogether, and simply work towards eating more plants and fewer animals).

2  DO YOUR RESEARCH

Knowledge is everything. If you're interested in veganism and what it stands for, then gather enough information so that you can fully understand what it's all about and why it's important to you. It's especially helpful to be armed with the knowledge when your family and friends start asking lots of questions about your new plant-based lifestyle.

3  READ THE LABEL

At first it can seem like a bit of a chore, but reading the labels of foods as a beginner is vital to understanding what's in your food. After a while, you'll get used to reading the labels, as well as knowing what foods do or don't contain animal products. Luckily allergens such as milk, egg and fish are usually highlighted in bold on the ingredients lists of products, but there are other less obvious items to look out for.

## Check food labels for:

Whey, casein, lactose, shellac, rennet, albumen, gelatine, food-grade wax, isinglass, lard, natural flavourings, vitamin D3 (unless labelled as vegan), carmine, anchovies, lactic acid, beeswax and certain E-numbers (you can find full lists of non-vegan E numbers online[58]).

4  VEGANISE YOUR FAVOURITE RECIPES

One of my top tips for those starting a vegan diet is to make vegan versions of your favourite non-vegan foods! Just because you're vegan now doesn't mean you can't enjoy a good pizza or burger. As you'll be taking out meat, dairy and eggs from your diet, at first it may feel like there's not much left to eat. But the key is finding new ways to eat what you're used to as you never want to feel restricted. There are lots of really easy and delicious recipes coming in this chapter, plus I have hundreds more on my YouTube channel and website. Whatever you fancy, all it takes is a quick Google search of your favourite meal, followed by the word 'vegan' and you'll find plenty of delicious recipes to recreate.

5  FIND ALTERNATIVES

Now this will inevitably vary depending on where you live, but in many countries there are plenty of vegan options on offer to try. When I first went vegan nearly six years ago, my only option was a sad, smelly vegan 'cheese' that tasted more like feet than my favourite cheddar. This gave me a bleak and cheese-less image of my future. But thankfully I learnt how to make my own (recipe on pages 191–193), and nowadays there are so many vegan cheeses available in the UK that taste like the real deal. It makes me so happy how popular veganism is becoming: it means there are more and more easily available options for lots of us to enjoy! If you don't have many alternatives local to you yet, then I'm going to teach you how to make your own in the following pages.

6  LEAD BY EXAMPLE

When you learn about the animal agriculture industry, what it is doing to animals, people and the planet, it can become hard not to get very mad about it. At the start, my passion for veganism ended in a few uncomfortable confrontations with the people close to me. What I've learnt along the way, however, is that leading by example works a lot better than getting into arguments. There is nothing wrong with a healthy discussion, if the other person wants to have it, but try your best to reserve that passion for other more positive uses. Show those around you how amazing vegan food tastes, share articles with them if they ask questions you feel you aren't sure of answering, speak calmly and positively when asked about veganism, and suggest documentaries or resources if anyone really grills you about your decision.

7   BE A PART OF THE COMMUNITY

This leads me to my next tip: get involved and find other likeminded people who you can talk to about veganism. Use your passion in ways that can make a difference. Join online forums, follow other vegans on social media, go to vegan meet-ups, potlucks, peaceful protests or activist events. One of the main reasons people give up veganism is because most people around us aren't vegan. Humans need community to thrive! Doing anything alone can be tricky, so make sure to find your vegan support system to help you through this lifestyle change.

8   GET CREATIVE

Plant-based cooking is a whole other world. While it may seem you're cutting a lot from your diet, you're opening a door to so many new tastes, spices, combinations and ingredients you've likely never tried before. I eat a much more varied diet since going vegan and I love it! The possibilities are truly endless when it comes to plants, so experiment, get creative and find what works for you.

9   ALLOW FOR MISTAKES

There isn't a vegan on this Earth who hasn't made a mistake. We live in a very non-vegan world, and so it's going to be easy to mess up – not to mention that when you're a beginner, you're still learning and finding your way. So allow for mistakes, get back up and start again. Just because you accidentally got served a milk in your coffee, or had a cheesy pizza after a night of drinking with your mates, doesn't mean you have to throw in the vegan towel. If your intentions are still there, and you're trying your best, then that's all that matters. Don't sweat the small stuff! Mistakes will happen less and less as you adjust and grow with this lifestyle.

10 NEVER RESTRICT

Going vegan means you'll be cutting out certain food groups from your diet. This will be a dramatic shift for most people's diets. Combat this by *swapping* foods, rather than cutting out any parts of your diet. For example, replace meat with plant-based proteins such as beans, legumes or vegan meat alternatives in your pasta or stir-fry, and use a plant-based milk in your tea or cereal. Learn more about nutrition and make sure that you're making smart decisions when it comes to eating a balanced vegan diet. Don't follow any vegan fad diets where there are any rules or restrictions.

If you are someone who is dealing with, or has dealt with any form of disordered eating or eating disorder, then a vegan diet might not be for you, and recovery should be your focus. Please speak to a registered dietician or healthcare professional if you are at all worried about getting all the right nutrients on a vegan diet, including supplementing effectively.

## 11 LEAVE EXPECTATIONS BEHIND AND DON'T GIVE UP

I couldn't leave it at just ten tips, so here is a bonus! In order to combat climate change, we've all got to change our diets. But we can't set high expectations on ourselves and others to be able to easily go vegan. Don't assume that veganism will be super-easy, help you lose weight, transform your health or give you the answers to everything. Leave behind any unrealistic expectations you have, and remember that veganism is fundamentally about *reducing the amount of harm you are causing the planet as an individual*. It isn't a fad diet, nor a miracle cure for health issues. It can take time to adjust as it's a big change in your diet, but that doesn't mean it can't be achieved. If you're finding that eating vegan is making you feel bloated, maybe take it easy and introduce vegan foods slowly over time. If you aren't feeling the health benefits, or losing weight, remember it isn't a 'diet' in the traditional sense, and shouldn't be treated as one. And if you find being completely vegan is too restrictive for you, then forget the label and endeavour to reduce in the ways *you* can. It's much more realistic for everyone to reduce animal products and give plant-based eating a go, than for everyone to go completely vegan. Find a way that is sustainable for you long term.

# Kitchen Staples

Now you're ready to think about your food choices, let's cover the basics of what you'll need to cook up a storm in the kitchen. You may have a lot of these items in your cupboards already, but hopefully these pantry and cupboard staples will help you to create delicious and easy plant-based meals, reduce your waste and eat as sustainably as possible. They're definitely not all a necessity, but they're a great selection to make delicious meals with every week. If you're after any of the equipment or utensils from the list, find out if your family or friends have spares, or if you can get lucky at your local charity shop!

EQUIPMENT AND UTENSILS

Measuring cups and spoons
Colander/sieve
Mixing bowls
Chopping boards
Wooden/metal spoons
Spatula
Measuring jug
Food grater/zester
Sharp knives (knife sharpener)
Whisk
Kitchen scale
Casserole dish
Large non-stick frying pan/wok
Baking dish
Teapot/tea infuser
Tofu press
Blender
Food processor
Reusable baking sheet

### RICE AND GRAINS

Basmati rice
Brown rice
Pasta
Noodles
Couscous
Bulgar wheat
Rolled oats/
porridge oats

### LEGUMES

Lentils
Chickpeas
Kidney beans
Black beans

### VEG

Onions
Garlic
Potatoes

### STORAGE/REUSABLES

Glass jars
Tupperware
Cotton/mesh produce bags
Reusable/travel cutlery

## SPICES AND SEASONING

Sea salt
Black pepper
Chilli powder/cayenne
Chilli flakes
Paprika
Cumin
Garam masala
Turmeric
Curry powder
Cinnamon
Nutmeg
Garlic powder
Bay leaf
Stock cubes
Nutritional yeast

## HERBS

Mixed herbs
Oregano
Thyme
Basil
Dil

## TINS AND CANS

Tinned tomatoes
Coconut milk
Tomato puree
Beans

FOOD AND DRINK

PANTRY

**OIL**

Olive oil
Vegetable oil
Sesame oil

**VINEGAR**

Balsamic vinegar
Cider vinegar
Red wine vinegar
Rice vinegar

**CONDIMENTS**

Soy sauce
Sriracha
Mustard
Ketchup
Brown sauce

**SUGAR AND SWEETENERS**

Light brown sugar
White granulated sugar
Caster sugar
Icing sugar
Maple syrup
Vanilla extract
Chocolate
Dark chocolate
Cocoa powder

**FLOUR**

Bread flour
Plain flour
Whole wheat

**YEAST**

Cornflour
Bicarbonate of soda and
baking powder

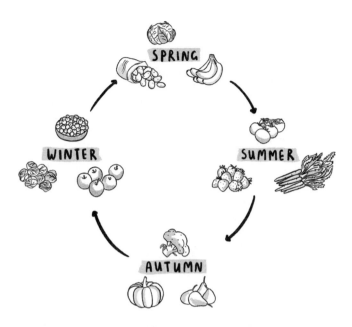

# Seasonal Food Guide

While a dietary shift is the biggest change you can make to your food footprint, buying locally and seasonally can also play a significant part in reducing the miles it takes for your food to get to your plate.[59] Eating locally has many benefits for the environment, including lowering carbon emissions, paying small-scale farmers and businesses, and supporting the local economy rather than big business multinationals. Food deserts, however, make it near impossible for some to eat locally-grown fresh foods, and instead they must rely on packaged and processed foods. So if you are in a lucky position where you *can* access fresh fruits and vegetables locally to you, try to make the most of this opportunity. Get onto Google, ask around, and keep your eyes peeled for farmers' markets and stalls near you. Support your local farmers and businesses and strengthen your local economy. Plus it'll taste a lot more fresh than the stuff from the supermarket! I've listed below different fruits and vegetables that are optimum to buy at certain times of the year, to reduce the food miles of your meal.

| | VEG | FRUIT |
|---|---|---|
| January | beetroot, Brussels sprouts, cauliflower, celeriac, celery, chicory, Jerusalem artichoke, kale, leeks, parsnips, potatoes, shallots, swede, turnips | apples, clementines, kiwi fruit, lemons, oranges, passionfruit, pomegranate, rhubarb, satsumas, tangerines |
| February | Brussels sprouts, cauliflower, celeriac, chicory, Jerusalem artichoke, kale, leeks, parsnips, potatoes, purple sprouting broccoli, shallots, swede, turnips | bananas, clementines, kiwi fruit, lemons, oranges, passionfruit, pineapple, pomegranate, rhubarb |
| March | cauliflower, celeriac, leeks, purple sprouting broccoli, spinach, spring onions, swede | bananas, kiwi fruit, lemons, oranges, passionfruit, pineapple, rhubarb |
| April | asparagus, broccoli, Jersey Royal new potatoes, lettuce, purple sprouting broccoli, radishes, rocket, spinach, spring onions | bananas, kiwi fruit, rhubarb |
| May | asparagus, broccoli, carrots, lettuce, new potatoes, peas, radishes, rocket, spinach, spring onions | bananas, kiwi fruit, rhubarb |
| June | artichoke, asparagus, aubergine, beetroot, broad beans, broccoli, carrots, courgettes, fennel, French beans, lettuce, mangetout, new potatoes, pak choi, peas, radishes, rocket, runner beans, spinach, spring onions, tomatoes, turnips | apricots, blueberries, cherries, gooseberries, kiwi fruits, peaches, strawberries |
| July | artichoke, aubergine, beetroot, broad beans, broccoli, carrots, courgettes, fennel, French beans, lettuce, mangetout, new potatoes, pak choi, peas, radishes, rocket, runner beans, spinach, spring onions, tomatoes, turnips | apricots, blueberries, cherries, gooseberries, kiwi fruit, melons, peaches, strawberries |

| | VEG | FRUIT |
|---|---|---|
| **August** | artichoke, aubergine, beetroot, broad beans, broccoli, carrots, courgettes, cucumber, fennel, French beans, lettuce, mangetout, marrow, mushrooms, pak choi, peas, peppers, potatoes, radishes, rocket, runner beans, spring onions, sweetcorn, tomatoes, turnips | apricot, blueberries, cherries, figs, loganberries, melons, nectarines, peaches, plums, raspberries, redcurrants, strawberries |
| **September** | artichoke, aubergine, beetroot, broccoli, carrots, celeriac, celery, courgette, fennel, French beans, kale, leeks, lettuce, mangetout, macro, mushrooms, pak choi, peppers, potatoes, pumpkin radishes, rocket, runner beans, shallots, spring onions, squash, sweetcorn, tomatoes, turnips | apples, blackberries, elderberries, figs, melons, nectarines, peaches, pears, plums, raspberries, redcurrant |
| **October** | artichoke, beetroot, broccoli, Brussels sprouts, butternut squash, celeriac, celery, chicory, fennel, kale leeks, lettuce, marrow, mushrooms, parsnips, potatoes, pumpkin, radishes, rocket, runner beans, shallots, swede, sweetcorn, tomatoes, turnips | apples, blackberries, elderberries, figs, grapes, pears, quince |
| **November** | artichoke, beetroot, Brussels sprouts, butternut squash, cauliflower, celeriac, celery, chicory, kale, leeks, mushrooms, parsnips, potatoes, pumpkin, shallots, swede, turnips | apples, clementines, cranberries, passionfruit, pears, pomegranate quince, satsumas, |
| **December** | beetroot, Brussels sprouts, cauliflower, celeriac, celery, chicory, Jerusalem artichoke, kale, leeks, mushrooms, parsnips, potatoes, shallots, swede, turnips | apples, clementines, cranberries, passionfruit, pears, pineapple, pomegranate, satsumas, tangerines |

# Ten Easy Tips to Reduce Food Waste:

1   MEAL PLAN AND PREP

Thinking ahead and getting organised about what you're making that week can dramatically reduce any food going to waste. We all have busy lives, but if you can fit in just a small part of each week to plan ahead and prepare the food you'll be eating during the week, you can save yourself some money and time in the long run.

Try planning 4–5 main meals for your week, taking into account what you already have in your cupboards. From there you can make a shopping list of ingredients, alongside any snacks or lunch foods you regularly eat. I usually stick to planning just the 4–5 meals as it accounts for leftovers, eating out, or having extra of anything towards the end of the week.

Once you have your meal plan, you can prep some of the foods in their entirety, or simply prep some ingredients that you can easily grab from your fridge to put together a tasty and healthy meal. Part of the reason we end up buying pre-packaged foods, or meals that don't make us feel our best, is due to convenience. So make it easier for yourself by making meals ahead of time at the weekend, and storing them in the fridge or freezer to reheat. Meal prepping healthy snacks such as energy bars or pre-cut veg, or cooking some sweet potato or tofu ahead of time, means that making quick lunches and dinners becomes a lot more convenient.

|  | MEAL | SHOPPING LIST |
|---|---|---|
| MON | | |
| TUES | | |
| WED | | |
| THURS | | |
| FRI | | |
| SAT | | |
| SUN | | |

2 STICK TO YOUR LIST AND USE WHAT YOU HAVE

Take your list to the shop with you and stick to it. You don't need the extra 'buy one get one free' offers, or the new product that the shop is promoting. And don't go shopping hungry!

3 BULK BUY

Bulk buying dry foods can lower your food waste because of the larger packages, resulting in less plastic (it's also usually cheaper overall). Find out if you have a shop near you which offers bulk ingredients that you can fill up in your own jars or bags without any packaging. Asian supermarkets, Indian grocery shops, green grocers, zero waste shops, bakeries are all places where you can buy in bulk. Rope in your family and friends and bulk buy wholesale food as a group to save on packaging and transportation.

4 LEARN HOW TO STORE YOUR FOOD

Understanding how long food will last will stop you from constantly throwing away foods that don't get eaten. Be prepared with air-tight jars and containers that can keep your food fresh for longer. Bread will last longest in a bread bin, out of sunlight, while carrots will last longest in some water in the fridge.

5 AVOID PEELING

I used to peel everything without thinking about it. But the skins of veg can still be eaten! Potato skins can make chips more rustic, carrots can simply be washed and the skin on ginger will just add even more flavour.

6 DON'T OVER-CONSUME

When we have access to so much food, we can easily over-consume on snacks, treats, deals and extras. Be aware of how much food you actually need and eat each week, so you aren't simply filling up your cupboards further and further every time you go shopping.

7  PANTRY/FRIDGE CHALLENGE

On a regular basis, try cleaning out your fridge and pantry of foods that have been sitting there a while and use up any leftovers. Get inventive and see what meals can be made out of the random ingredients you bought for one recipe that you never used again. This will not only reduce your monthly food spending, but make sure that no food in your cupboards or fridge goes to waste. Resist that urge to go shopping when you probably already have the ingredients in your cupboards to use up.

8  COMPOST

When you have to throw food away, try composting instead of chucking it in the normal bin. At least that way the food can go back into nature. You can use it for your garden, or donate it to a local garden near you that needs it. Check pages 248–251 for more information on how to compost.

9  EAT/ORDER OUT LESS

Regularly eating out at restaurants or cafes and ordering takeaway are inevitably very wasteful, from the large portions we don't manage to eat, to the plastic packaging that comes with it. Make eating out or ordering a takeaway a treat, rather than a habit.

10 AVOID THROWING AWAY

We throw away so much food without thinking about how it could be used in another way. Keep your leftover dinners, even if it's just a small amount, and enjoy the next day for lunch (or freeze for another day!). If bread is going hard, blend it up into breadcrumbs and store in the freezer. When your food is coming close to its sell-by date, freeze it. Shove any over-ripe fruits or saggy vegetables into a smoothie or juice. Get creative and try to find a way to use that food before it goes in the bin.

# Get the most out of your food

### OVERRIPE BANANAS

Make some yummy banana bread or pancakes, or break
them up and put in the freezer for smoothies another day!

### STALE BREAD

Slice and pop in the freezer for toast, or pulse in a food processor
and store in your freezer to use as breadcrumbs in a recipe.

### OLD VEGETABLES

Freeze these and use them in my vegetable
stock recipe on page 189.

### MILK

Know how much milk you drink so it doesn't get poured
down the sink, or try making your own (recipe on page 190).
If you have a plant milk that needs using up, add it to smoothies,
stir-fries, make a hot chocolate or a creamy pasta sauce.

### POTATOES

Store them in a dark place and parboil potatoes that need to
be used then store in the freezer for when you need them!

### APPLES

Keep your apples away from your other fruit to stop them going
off quicker, and keep them out of the sun and in a dark dry
place! If they need to be eaten, slice them up and bake them in
a small dish topped with oats, sugar, cinnamon, nuts and raisins.

# Cooking From Scratch

Now your pantry and cupboards are fully stocked, you're a whizz at storing and not wasting your food, let's get cooking! Below are some delicious yet easy recipes that you can add to your arsenal to adapt and recreate using whatever you have in your fridge, what's seasonal and what you enjoy.

BASICS
Bread
Nut butters
Vegetable stock
Plant milk
Almond cheese
Cashew cheese sauce
Nut-free cheese
Vegan butter

MAIN MEALS
Easy breakfast porridge
Granola
Muesli
Tofu scramble
Seasonal stir-fry
High-protein stew/chilli
Winter soup
Creamy one-pot pasta
Easy vegetable curry
Black bean burger

SNACKS
Homemade crisps
Roasted chickpeas
Chocolate truffles

SAUCES/DIPS
Tomato ketchup
Pesto
Hummus
Salsa

DRINKS
Hot chocolate
Smoothies

# Bread

makes 2 small loafs, 1 large loaf or 24 rolls

I recently started making my own bread and it's so satisfying and rewarding to do! Plus, it's super cheap, saves on the packaging that bread usually comes in, and can be made in a huge variety of ways.

INGREDIENTS

3 x 7g sachets fast-action yeast
2 tbsp sugar
450ml/16floz (1¾ cups) lukewarm water
500g/18oz (4 cups) white or wholemeal strong bread flour
500g/18oz (4 cups) plain flour, plus extra for dusting
25g salt
Oil for greasing

METHOD

1  Add the yeast and sugar to the water, mix well and leave for around 5–10 minutes, until it activates.
2  Combine the flours and salt in a large bowl.
3  If using a food mixer with a dough hook, add the dry ingredients with the yeast mixture and mix on medium to high speed for approximately 3–4 minutes, until everything has come together to form an elastic dough, then continue from step 5.
4  If you don't have a food mixer, make a well in the centre of your dry ingredients and slowly add the yeast and water mixture into the middle of the well, bringing in the flour to form a sticky mixture.
5  Turn the dough out onto a lightly floured surface and start kneading with the ball of your palm by pushing the mixture away from you and folding it back for around 5–10 minutes, until you form an elastic dough.
6  Place your dough in a lightly oiled bowl, cover with a damp cloth and leave to prove until it has doubled in size (around half an hour to 1 hour). A good test is to poke the dough with your finger, and if it springs back, it is ready. Ideally prove your dough in a warm corner of your house.

7   Now it has done its first prove, you can knock it back with
    your hands, removing the air and kneading for a couple
    more minutes.

8   Form the desired shape for your bread: a large round ball,
    separate rolls, in a loaf tin, whatever you like. Cover, and leave to
    prove again for a further 30 minutes to an hour or until it has
    doubled in size. This step can be left out if you're short on time.

9   Preheat your oven to 200°C, 400°F, gas mark 6 and gently place
    your bread onto a lightly floured baking tray and bake in the
    oven for 25–30 minutes (this depends on your oven). Make sure
    to close the door gently and keep an eye on the bread in the
    last 10 minutes so that it is perfectly brown. To test whether the
    bread is ready, gently tap the bottom of the loaf and if it sounds
    hollow it's done. If it doesn't then it needs a little longer to bake.
    Once cooked, leave to cool on a rack for 30 minutes.

## Easy swap

TINNED FOODS OVER PLASTIC PACKAGED FOODS
Explore the supermarket and find what foods you can
find in a tin that can be recycled, over in a plastic bag that
can't. Not only this, but tinned foods last a lot longer in
your cupboard and therefore will reduce on food waste.

## Nut butters

Making your own nut butters is super simple! They're a yummy spread on toast, on top of porridge or as a delicious dip with fruit. You can do this with any nuts you like, and you can also blend a variety of nuts into one butter. Peanuts, almonds, hazelnuts or walnuts are a great place to start when it comes to nut butters.

INGREDIENTS

300g /10oz (2 cups)
    nuts such as peanuts,
    almonds, hazelnuts
    or walnuts
A pinch of sea salt

**Optional additions:**
1-2 tbsp chia seeds
1-2 tbsp hemp seeds
1-2 tbsp cocoa powder
1/2 tsp vanilla

METHOD

1 Preheat your oven to 180°C, 350°F, gas mark 4 and pour the nuts onto a baking tray. Roast in the oven for 8–12 minutes, keeping an eye on them in the last few minutes to make sure they don't burn.

2 If using hazelnuts, once baked, remove from the baking tray and rub inside a towel to remove the skins (not all the skin will come off, but try removing as much as possible).

3 Add the nuts to a food processor and blend until creamy and smooth. This will take time, with the nuts crumbling at first, and then releasing the oils to turn into a creamy nut butter. It should take around 10 minutes to fully blend (though this time will vary depending on the power of your food processor).

4 Once blended, feel free to add salt to taste. Or if using the add-ins such as chia or flax, add these now.

5 Transfer your nut butter to an air-tight jar and store in the fridge for up to 3–4 weeks.

*Vegan Nutella!*

Make your hazelnut butter following the above recipe. Once blended, add in 1–3 tbsp maple syrup (or other sweetener) to taste, 1–2 tbsp cocoa powder and a dash of plant milk until you reach the desired consistency.

# Vegetable stock

A great way to save on waste in the kitchen is to keep all odds and ends of vegetables to make them into a stock. Ends and skins of onion, garlic, celery, carrots, leeks, potatoes, mushrooms, herbs and any other veggies you have used throughout the week will add great flavour to a homemade stock. Try to avoid cruciferous vegetables such as cabbage, broccoli, Brussels sprouts or cauliflower that may leave a bitter taste to your broth. Save your veg in a container and freeze them until you have enough to make some yummy vegetable stock.

INGREDIENTS
A dash of oil
2 onions, chopped
5 garlic cloves, chopped
3 carrots, chopped
2 sticks celery, chopped
2–3 cups frozen vegetable scraps
A handful of fresh herbs or a sprinkle of dried herbs
2.5 litres/4.5 pints water
1 tsp salt
1 tsp black pepper

METHOD
1 Heat the oil in a large pan or casserole dish and cook the onion, garlic, carrots and celery, until softened.
2 Add in your vegetable scraps and herbs and stir through for a couple of minutes.
3 Pour over the water and bring to a boil. Reduce and simmer for 1 hour. Season to taste.
4 Strain broth through a cloth or sieve and leave to cool. Compost the vegetable scraps.
5 Store in an airtight jar for up to a week in the fridge or freeze in smaller portions to use later.

# Plant milk

Plant milks are another great alternative to make from scratch at home, while saving on waste. This recipe works for nuts (such as almonds), oats or rice.

INGREDIENTS

150g/6oz (1 cup) nuts/oats/white rice
500–750ml/1–1½ pints (2–3 cups) water
A pinch of sea salt
2 dates/1 tbsp maple syrup *(optional)*

METHOD

1 Soak the nuts, oats or rice in the cold water overnight.
2 Drain, rinse thoroughly and blend in a high-speed blender with 1 litre/ 1¾ pints (4 cups) of water and a pinch of salt. Feel free to sweeten with a couple of dates or maple syrup if you like.
3 Strain twice if too much residue is left in the milk
4 Once fully blended (this may take quite a few minutes depending on your blender), pour the liquid through a nut milk bag or muslin bag (or simply a thin tea towel over a sieve into a bowl if you don't have these). Squeeze out the remaining liquid until all has dripped through.
5 Pour the milk into a jar and keep in the fridge for around 4–5 days.

*Top tip!*

Keep the pulp in a container in the fridge or freezer and use in baking energy bars, add to your oats in the morning, or use it to bake some cookies or muffins.

# Vegan Cheese

## Almond cheese

Tasty vegan cheese can be hard to come by depending on where you live, so why not make your own? This almond cheese is full of flavour and works perfectly spread on crackers.

INGREDIENTS
- 75g/3oz (½ cup) almonds
- 1 small garlic clove
- 2 tbsp coconut oil
- 4 tbsp nutritional yeast
- 1 tsp mixed herbs
- Juice of ½ lemon
- ½ tsp sugar
- 1 tsp salt
- Pinch of pepper

METHOD
1. Soak the nuts in cold water overnight, or in boiling water for an hour.
2. Drain and rinse the nuts. Add to a food processor or blender with the rest of the ingredients. Pour in 80ml/3fl oz (⅓ cup) water.
3. Blend to your desired texture and creaminess (you may need to stop and scrape the edges of the blender a few times).
4. Leave to cool, spoon into a bowl or container, then set in the fridge for 1–2 hours.
5. Store in the fridge in an air-tight container for up to a week.

## Cashew cheese sauce

Try mixing this cheese sauce into pasta or load it on top of nachos for a delicious plant-based alternative to cheese.

INGREDIENTS
75g/3oz (½ cup) cashews
1 small garlic clove
250ml/9fl oz (1 cup) plant milk
30g/1oz (½ cup) nutritional yeast
½ tsp chilli flakes
¼ tsp paprika
Juice of ½ lemon
½ tsp salt
Pinch of pepper
Chopped jalapeños for topping

METHOD
1 Soak the nuts in cold water overnight, or in boiling water for an hour.
2 Drain and rinse the nuts, then add to a food processor or blender with the rest of the ingredients except the jalapenos.
3 Blend until smooth and saucy, pour into a bowl and top with jalapenos.
4 Eat warm or leave to cool. Store in the fridge in an air-tight container for up to a week.

# Nut-free cheese

For those of you with a nut allergy, here is a vegan nut-free cheese packed with flavour and nutrition.

INGREDIENTS

**Cheese mixture:**
45g/1.5oz (½ cup) oats
1 small garlic clove
1 tbsp coconut oil, plus
    extra for greasing
1 small cooked
    sweet potato
4 tbsp nutritional yeast
1 tbsp cornflour
½ tsp paprika

1 tsp sugar
Juice of ½ lemon
1 tsp salt
Pinch of pepper
125ml/4 ½fl oz
    (½ cup) water

**Agar mixture:**
1½ tsp agar agar powder

METHOD
1   Blend all the main cheese ingredients in a high-speed blender until thick, smooth and creamy.
2   For the agar mixture, bring 250ml/9fl oz (1 cup) water to the boil in a pan. Lower the temperature and add the agar agar, stirring continuously until the mixture has thickened up.
3   Add the blended ingredients to the pan and stir for another minute.
4   Pour mixture into a lightly oiled bowl or tin to set.
5   Leave to cool (without a lid), and then set in the fridge for 1–2 hours. Turn the dish upside down and enjoy sliced or grated! Store in the fridge in air-tight container for up to a week.

*Top tip!*
   If you aren't allergic to nuts, try this recipe with cashews instead of oats, using the same measurement and soaking them ahead of time.

# Vegan butter

I've recently started to make my own vegan butter from scratch as it's super simple, keeps for a long time in the fridge and is free from dairy, plastic and palm oil!

INGREDIENTS

1 tsp apple cider vinegar
80ml/3fl oz (⅓ cup) unsweetened plant milk
200g/7oz (1 cup) coconut oil *(refined if possible)*
2 tsp nutritional yeast
Pinch of turmeric
½ tsp salt
2 tbsp extra virgin olive oil

METHOD

1 Prepare a mould for the butter to go in – a butter dish of course works perfectly, but any dish you like can be used.
2 Add the apple cider vinegar into the plant milk and whisk to curdle it together. Let it sit for 10 minutes or so until it has curdled.
3 Melt the coconut oil a little in the microwave or on the stove top – don't get it too hot: as close to room temperature as possible.
4 Add the coconut oil, nutritional yeast, turmeric and salt to a food processor or blender and blend until fully mixed, scraping down the sides as needed.
5 Stir in the olive oil and pour into the mould. Place in the freezer to set. This should take around 1 hour.
6 Use the butter as you would normal butter, on toast, in sandwiches or to cook and bake with. Store in the fridge in an air-tight container for up to one month.

# Main Meals

......................................................................................................

## Easy breakfast porridge serves 1

Porridge (or oats) is a staple in our household. Mainly because it's a) super easy, b) absolutely delicious, c) easily adaptable to any season, flavour or craving, d) filling, e) totally good for you. The basic ratio for perfect stove-top oats is 1 part oats, to 2 parts liquid. I like to use half water and half plant milk for my porridge to make it nice and creamy. Adjust the amount of oats depending on your appetite and add whatever fruits and flavours you enjoy the most!

INGREDIENTS
    50–100g/2–4oz (½–1 cup) oats
    125–250ml/4½–9fl oz (½–1 cup) water
    125–250ml/4½ – 9fl oz (½–1 cup) plant milk

**Flavour or sweetener:**
1 tsp cinnamon
1 tbsp maple syrup
    or 1 tsp brown sugar
    or 1 chopped
    medjool date
Fruits of your choice

**Optional additions:**
1 tbsp chia or flax seeds
1 tbsp cocoa powder
Dollop of nut butter

METHOD
1  Pour the oats and liquids into a pan over low to medium heat and stir through.
2  If using (which I recommend), add in the cinnamon and sweetener and stir through.
3  At this point you can also add your fruit, such as a banana, an apple or some berries. I alternate whether I cook the fruit with the porridge, add it on top, or both. Similarly, if using chia or flax seeds for some healthy fats, or cocoa powder to make chocolate porridge, add this in now.

4  Keep stirring the porridge over low to medium heat, making sure it doesn't come to a boil or cook too fast. Cook until the liquid is absorbed and you have reached your desired texture. Cook for less time if you prefer runny oats, or for longer if you prefer them a little thicker.

5  Pour into your bowl and add any extra toppings, such as chopped fruit, maple syrup or a dollop of nut butter, and enjoy!

*Top tip!*

No time to cook your breakfast in the mornings? Try overnight oats! Use the same ingredients, except the water (I usually add in a tbsp or two of chia seeds), mix in a jar and store in the fridge overnight. Top with some of your favourite additions such as fruit or a dollop of nut butter and enjoy on the go in the morning.

## Easy swap

LOOSE LEAF TEA OVER TEA BAGS
Most tea bags contain plastic and therefore can't be composted.

# Granola

Homemade granola always beats store bought; it's also super
simple and you can easily adapt to make it your own!

INGREDIENTS

    4 tbsp coconut oil
    150g/5oz (½ cup) maple syrup
    1 tsp vanilla extract
    180g/7oz (2 cups) oats
    150g/5oz (1 cup) nuts of your choice
    60g/2oz (½ cup) seeds
    150g/5oz (1 cup) dried fruit of your choice

METHOD

1   Preheat your oven to 160°C, 320°F, gas mark 3.
2   Melt the oil, maple syrup and vanilla in a saucepan for a couple
    of minutes.
3   Mix the dry ingredients, apart from the dried fruit, together in a
    large bowl. Pour over the melted wet ingredients and combine.
4   Spread evenly onto a lined baking tray and bake for 20–25
    minutes, or until golden brown. If you like crumbly granola,
    stir midway. If you prefer chunky granola, then simply turn the
    baking tray midway without touching the granola to ensure
    everything is evenly baked. Keep an eye on it towards the end so
    it doesn't burn and remove once golden brown.
5   Remove from the oven, add in the dried fruit, and allow to
    completely cool. Store in an air-tight container for up to two
    weeks (but I'd be impressed if it lasted that long as mine's usually
    gobbled up within a day or two!). Enjoy as a snack on its own,
    or with some plant milk and fruit for a delicious breakfast.

# Muesli

Similar to granola, muesli is another great staple to make your own at home. Use your favourite nuts, seeds and dried fruits, and try out different combinations to make it your own!

INGREDIENTS

    180g/6oz (2 cups) oats
    1 tbsp chia seeds
    1 tbsp flax seeds
    2 tbsp mixed seeds *(pumpkin and sunflower are my go-to)*
    90g/3.5oz (½ cup) dried dates, chopped
    75g/3oz (½ cup) raisins
    50g/2oz (½ cup) desiccated coconut
    2 tsp cinnamon

METHOD

Simply mix all the ingredients together, adapting to your preferences, and store in an air-tight container for up to two months.

# Tofu scramble

serves 2–3

If you prefer a savoury breakfast, tofu scramble is a great alternative to scrambled eggs for breakfast. I also enjoy making tofu scramble for lunch and dinner with some added spice, served with rice or potatoes.

INGREDIENTS

A dash of oil
½ red onion, chopped
1 garlic clove, crushed
1 tsp turmeric
½ tsp cumin
Your choice of veg – for example, tomatoes or red pepper
    *(optional)*
1 x 400g block firm tofu
1–2 tbsp soy sauce
Salt and pepper
Handful of baby spinach *(optional)*

METHOD

1  Heat the oil in a frying pan over a medium heat and cook the onion until softened.
2  Add the garlic with the spices and fry for a minute or two.
3  If using veg like pepper or tomatoes, finely chop and add in here. Use a dash of water if needed.
4  Crumble in the block of tofu with your hands to create the scrambled 'egg' texture. Stir through the soy sauce, salt and pepper and fry for around 5 minutes until everything is cooked.
5  If using spinach, add this in now until wilted.
6  Serve over toast for breakfast, or alongside other grains or potatoes any time of the day!

# Seasonal stir-fry

serves 2–3

We love a good stir-fry in our house, and it's always what I make when I have no time and want something delicious and nutritious. The basic element of stir-fry always remains the same, but I always change the veg depending on what I have in the fridge, or what is in season. So, try out different combinations throughout the year!

INGREDIENTS

Packet noodles *(whatever type you like, and however much you like)*
A dash of oil
1 red onion, chopped
2–3 garlic cloves, crushed
Thumb of ginger, peeled and chopped
1 chilli, finely chopped
Seasonal vegetables *(some of my favourite to use are peppers, mushrooms, broccoli, spinach, kale, courgette, green beans, sugar snap peas – think about combining different textures, sweetnesses and add something green in there too)*
Juice of 1 lemon or lime
Handful of chopped coriander
Sprinkling of sesame seeds

**Sauce:**
2 tbsp soy sauce
1 tbsp maple syrup
1 tbsp apple cider vinegar
Juice of a lemon or lime

**For peanut satay** *(optional)*:
2 tbsp peanut butter
*(use tahini if you're allergic to nuts)*
400ml tin coconut milk

**Optional additions:**
Tofu
1 tbsp sriracha

METHOD

1  If using tofu, drain, press and cut into cubes.
2  Cook the noodles as per packet instructions. Keep an eye on this as you follow the next steps and when cooked, drain and thoroughly rinse through cold water. Return to the pan on the side for when you need it (unless using instant or rice noodles, in which case you can add these to the pan when you add the sauce ingredients).
3  Meanwhile, heat a dash of oil in a large wok or large frying pan over medium to high heat. Add in the onion and fry until softened.
4  Add in the garlic, ginger and chilli and cook for a few more minutes, stirring continuously.
5  If using tofu add this now, and fry for around 5 minutes.
6  Next add the vegetables into the pan. Keep frying, adding a dash of water if it needs it.
7  Now to add the sauce ingredients! I never measure these, but rather go by eye and taste. The measurements above are therefore a guide that you can try out and adapt to your own taste. Depending on how many vegetables or what type I will add in more soy sauce, or I'll add in some extra spice with some sriracha depending on how spicy the chilli is.
8  Cook for around 5–10 minutes, until all the vegetables are cooked, and the sauce is incorporated.
9  Finally, stir in the cooked noodles to warm through and cover in the sauce and veg. Serve with a sprinkle of coriander, sesame seeds and some lemon or lime wedges!

*Top tip!*

For a peanut satay stir-fry add the peanut butter and coconut milk when adding the rest of the sauce ingredients.

# High-protein stew/chilli

Chilli and stew are amazing foods to make ahead of time as meal prep. I make chilli all the time as it is not only delicious but full of protein and so easy to prepare. I have made this recipe even higher in protein with some extra lentils, as well as adding in a little more liquid to give it a more stew-like consistency. If you prefer a thicker chilli, then leave out the vegetable stock. This can be enjoyed with rice, on top of a jacket potato or with some crusty bread as a soup.

INGREDIENTS

400g tin kidney beans/125g dried kidney beans
400g tin chickpeas/125g dried chickpeas
A dash of oil
1 onion, chopped
3 garlic cloves, crushed
1 red chilli, finely chopped
1 tsp each of cinnamon and cumin
1–2 tsp each paprika and chilli *(adjust according to preference)*
1 red pepper, deseeded and chopped
1 yellow pepper, deseeded and chopped *(or any other veg you like
    – I often add what I have in the fridge at the time, e.g. carrots or
    courgettes work really well finely chopped or grated)*
100g/4oz dry lentils
500ml/18fl oz (2 cups) vegetable stock *(see page 189)*
2 x 400ml tins chopped tomatoes
2 tbsp tomato puree
Salt and pepper

**Serve with:**
Cooked rice or potatoes
Bread
Sliced or diced avocado or guacamole
Lemon or lime juice
Fresh coriander

METHOD

1   If using dried beans and peas, soak in water overnight. Drain and tip into a large pan. Cover with cold water, bring to a boil and simmer for 45 minutes to an hour or until tender. Drain and rinse them ahead of making your chilli. If using tins of cooked beans then skip this step.

2   Heat the oil in a large pan or casserole dish. Add the onions and cook until softened.

3   Add the garlic and chilli and fry for a few minutes.

4   Add in the spices and mix, pouring in a dash of water to form a paste. Fry for a couple of minutes.

5   Next add the peppers and stir through.

6   Rinse the lentils and add to the pan along with the prepared stock, drained beans and chickpeas, tomatoes, puree and stir together. Bring to a boil, then turn down and simmer for 35–40 minutes.

7   When the chilli is reduced and cooked through, give it a taste, season with salt and pepper and adjust seasoning according to your preference, adding some extra spice if it needs it. If using coriander, thinly chop this up and add the stalks to the pan, reserving the leaves. Stir through.

8   Serve with your rice, potatoes or bread, some avocado or guacamole, the juice of a lemon or lime and the reserved chopped coriander leaves.

*Top tip!*

Add kale or spinach to this dish for some extra greens! Or bake some sweet potato in the oven and stir through for some sweetness.

# Winter soup

serves 2–3

There's nothing better during the winter months than a warming bowl of soup with some crusty bread. This recipe can, of course, be adapted to whatever seasonal vegetables you like, but I have suggested squash or cauliflower as the base to this as they are easy to get at this time of year and taste incredible in a soup!

INGREDIENTS

Head of cauliflower or 1 squash
A dash of oil
1 onion, chopped
1 leek, chopped
2 garlic cloves, crushed
Thumb of ginger, peeled and chopped
1 carrot, peeled and chopped
1 litre/1.75 pints (4 cups) vegetable stock *(see page 189)*
2 tbsp tomato puree
Salt and pepper

METHOD

1 Preheat your oven to 200°C, 400°F, gas mark 6.
2 If using cauliflower, break up into florets and place onto a lined baking tray, drizzle with oil, season and pop in the oven for 20–25 minutes, turning midway. If using squash (butternut or pumpkin), slice in half, remove the pulp and seeds, drizzle over some oil, season and bake with the centre facing upwards on a baking tray in the oven for 45 minutes.
3 Remove the squash or cauliflower from the oven to cool.
4 In a large pan, fry the onion and leek until softened in some oil.
5 Add in the garlic, ginger and carrots and continue frying for a few more minutes.
6 Add in your cauliflower or squash (you can either roughly chop this or spoon out from the skin) and pour over the stock. Stir through and bring to the boil.
7 Remove from the heat and either serve chunky, or blend until smooth (I use an immersion or hand blender for this).
8 Season with salt and pepper to taste and serve with crusty bread.

# Creamy one-pot pasta

serves 4

This is a perfect lazy meal for when you can't be bothered to use and wash lots of dishes. As always, the vegetable combos can be adjusted, or you could switch out the tahini for a tin of chopped tomatoes and 2 tbsp of tomato puree for a creamy tomato pasta. You can also experiment with a variety of pasta shapes, such as linguine or spaghetti!

INGREDIENTS

1 tbsp oil
1 onion, chopped
4 garlic cloves, crushed
Half a head of
    broccoli, trimmed
300g/10oz
    mushrooms, cleaned
500ml/18fl oz (2 cups)
    plant milk
2–3 tbsp tahini
500g/18fl oz (2 cups)
    water
500g/18oz penne pasta

Pinch of chilli flakes
Salt and pepper
Mixed dried herbs
30g/1oz (½ cup)
    nutritional yeast
Handful of fresh parsley
Juice of 1 lemon
100g/4oz (⅔ cups)
    frozen peas
100g/4oz spinach

METHOD

1   Heat the oil in a large frying pan or casserole dish and cook the onion and garlic until softened.

2   Chop up the broccoli and mushrooms and add to the pan. Stir and fry until the mushrooms have reduced.

3   Add in the milk, tahini, water, pasta, chilli flakes, salt, pepper, mixed herbs and nutritional yeast. Stir through and bring the mixture to a boil.

4   Once boiling, reduce and simmer for around 8–10 minutes, or until the pasta is al dente and the veggies tender.

5   Finely chop the parsley and add to the pan with the juice of a lemon, frozen peas and spinach. Stir through to cook for 1–2 minutes more.

6   Taste and adjust the seasoning and serve!

# Easy vegetable curry

serves 4

Curry is my absolute favourite food. There are so many different versions from all over the world, so it's difficult to share just the one recipe. That's why I've created a basic recipe that can be easily altered.

As a general rule of thumb, I always start my curries with an onion, some garlic and ginger. I will then add my spices, such as garam masala, cumin, chilli, turmeric and/or coriander. From there you can use a variety of vegetables such as aubergine, potatoes, peppers, mushrooms, broccoli, cauliflower or courgette (basically any vegetable). I also love to use tofu or beans like chickpeas in curry. Chopped tomatoes and coconut milk are my go-to for the sauce, and I sometimes also use a bit of vegetable stock. Finally, coriander and lemon juice are the perfect finishing touch to any curry.

INGREDIENTS

400g tin chickpeas/125g dried chickpeas or 400g block tofu
1 onion, chopped
3 garlic cloves, crushed
Thumb of ginger, peeled and chopped
1 chilli, deseeded and finely chopped
A dash of oil
Vegetables *(e.g. aubergine, courgette, mushrooms, broccoli, red pepper or a potato)*
1 tsp turmeric
1 tsp cumin
1 tsp garam masala
1 tsp ground coriander
400ml tin coconut milk
400ml tin chopped tomatoes
Salt and pepper
Small bunch of fresh coriander

**Serve with:**
Rice
Lemon juice

METHOD

1 If using dried chickpeas, soak in water overnight. Drain the chickpeas and tip into a pan. Cover with cold water, bring to a boil and simmer for 45 minutes to an hour or until tender. Drain and rinse them ahead of making your curry. If using tinned chickpeas then skip this step.

2 Add the onion, garlic, ginger and chilli to a large pan along with a dash of oil and cook until softened.

3 Meanwhile chop up the vegetables you're using into bite-sized chunks. Drain and rinse the chickpeas, or drain, press and cube the tofu.

4 Add the spices into the pan, adding a splash of water to loosen it up and create a paste. Fry for 1–2 minutes.

5 Add in the vegetables and chickpeas or tofu, stir through and fry for a few more minutes.

6 Pour in the coconut milk and tinned tomatoes and bring to a boil. Reduce to simmer and cook for 15–20 minutes until the sauce has thickened and reduced.

7 Season with salt and pepper, taste the curry and adjust spices to your liking if it needs it.

8 Chop the coriander, adding the stalks into the pan and keeping the leaves until later, stirring through.

9 Serve with rice, a sprinkle of coriander leaves, and a squeeze of lemon juice.

# Black bean burger

Just because you're eating something plant-based doesn't mean you have to miss out on the good ol' classics like a juicy burger! This black bean burger is one of my faves, as it's so full of flavour and feels as meaty as the real deal.

INGREDIENTS

400g tin black beans or
   125g dried black beans
1 flax egg (1 tbsp flaxmeal,
   3 tbsp water)
90g/3oz (1 cup)
   breadcrumbs
½ red onion, thinly sliced
200g/7oz (1 cup) cooked
   brown rice
1 tsp paprika
1 tsp cumin
½–1 tsp chilli
2 tsp garlic powder
2 tbsp Cornflour
Salt and pepper
1 tbsp balsamic vinegar
Olive oil for frying

**Burger sauce:**
1 tbsp vegan mayo
1 tbsp tomato sauce
½ tbsp sriracha
½ tsp Dijon mustard

**Serve with:**
Vegan cheese
Burger bun
Pickles
Lettuce

METHOD

1   If using dried black beans, soak in water overnight. Drain the beans and tip into a pan. Cover with cold water, bring to a boil and simmer for 45 minutes to an hour or until tender. Drain and rinse them ahead of making your burger. If using tinned black beans then skip this step.

2   Drain and rinse your beans and mash with hands, a potato masher or hand blender in a large bowl.

3   Prepare the flax egg by mixing the flax and water together in a bowl and leaving in the fridge to set. It's ready when it has come together to form a gloopy, egg-like texture.

4   Add the breadcrumbs to the beans along with the remaining
    ingredients (except the olive oil) and flax egg from the fridge.
    Mix together thoroughly (this can be done with your hands, or
    in a food processor).

5   Mould the burgers into four patties (this does take time as it'll
    be dry but keep pressing).

6   Refrigerate for a minimum of 10 minutes to allow them to set,
    making them easier to cook.

7   Mix the ingredients of the burger sauce together in a bowl and
    prepare your toppings.

8   Heat some olive oil in a pan over a high heat. Add the burgers
    and fry on either side for around 5–10 minutes, or until
    fully browned.

9   When the burgers are nearly done, add a slice of vegan cheese
    on top of each patty and cover with a lid until the cheese melts.

10  Toast the burger buns in a pan for a minute or two on each side
    *(optional)*.

11  Layer your burger buns up with the burger sauce, the burger,
    pickles and lettuce. Dig in and enjoy!

*Top tip!*

Freeze the patties for later use. They can be enjoyed as a part of
a buddha bowl, broken up with salad or in a sandwich.

## Easy swap

### THIN PLASTIC VS HARD PLASTIC

Plastic can't always be avoided, so look out for harder
plastics, or extra layers of plastics compared to one
layer of thinner plastics, or plastics you know can
be recycled. Choose the lesser of two evils.

# Snacks

## Homemade crisps

INGREDIENTS
- 1 potato
- 1 carrot
- 1 sweet potato
- 1 beetroot
- Olive oil
- 1 tsp salt

**Optional seasoning:**
- ½ tsp chilli flakes
- 1 tsp mixed herbs

METHOD
1. Preheat the oven to 150°C, 300°F, gas mark 2.
2. Wash your veg and then slice with a mandolin or the thick slicer on a grater. Make sure to slice them at an angle so they are long pieces, as they will shrink significantly in the oven.
3. Place them evenly on a lined baking tray, making sure they don't overlap, and drizzle with a little olive oil.
4. Bake in the oven for around 2 hours, removing when they are dry and crisp.
5. Sprinkle over the salt (and other seasoning you like) and serve hot or cold. Store in an air-tight container for a week.

# Roasted chickpeas

If you haven't already gathered, I adore chickpeas. And roasting them makes them crunchy and packed full of flavour.

INGREDIENTS

2 x 400g tins of chickpeas or 250g dried chickpeas
½ tsp each cumin, paprika, chilli, garlic powder
Olive oil
Juice of 1 lemon
Salt and pepper

METHOD

1   If using dried chickpeas, soak in water overnight. Drain the chickpeas and tip into a pan. Cover with cold water, bring to a boil and simmer for 45 minutes to an hour or until tender. If using tinned chickpeas then skip this step.
2   Preheat the oven to 200°C, 400°F, gas mark 6.
3   Drain and rinse the chickpeas and add to a bowl.
4   Add in the spices along with a drizzle of olive oil and the lemon juice. Season.
5   Pour onto a baking tray and bake in the oven for 30–40 minutes, shaking and turning occasionally until they are dry and crispy.

# Chocolate truffles

Who doesn't love a good truffle? The example below is for salted caramel truffles. However, over the Christmas period I make chocolate orange and coconut versions of this recipe. For chocolate orange, leave out the salt and simply zest an orange into your melted chocolate mixture, saving a little to sprinkle on top. For the coconut version, also leave out the salt and instead add 1 tbsp of desiccated coconut to the filling and sprinkle some extra on top of the melted chocolate.

INGREDIENTS

150g/5oz (1 cup) cashews
180g/6oz (1 cup) pitted medjool or halawi dates
2 tbsp cocoa powder
¼ tsp cinnamon
½ tsp vanilla extract
2 tbsp brown sugar
½ tsp sea salt *(plus extra for sprinkling)*

**For the coating:**
100g/4oz (⅔ cup) dark chocolate
½ tsp coconut oil

METHOD

1 Soak the cashews in bowl of boiling water for 15 minutes to soften.
2 Add the pitted dates to a food processor along with the drained cashews.
3 Add the remaining ingredients and blend until it all comes together. Scrape down the sides of the food processor midway to make sure everything is mixed thoroughly as it tends to stick.
4 Remove the caramel dough from the food processor and separate and roll evenly into 12–15 balls, depending on what size you want.
5 Leave to set in the freezer for 15 minutes.

6 When the truffles are set, add the dark chocolate to a heatproof bowl over a pan of simmering water. Stir the dark chocolate continuously until all the pieces are very nearly melted.

7 Remove from the heat and stir in the coconut oil.

8 Prepare a surface with some parchment paper ready for your truffles.

9 Move swiftly and dunk each individual truffle into the chocolate and leave to set on the parchment paper. I used two forks to do this so the chocolate could drip off easily. Once each truffle has been dipped in chocolate, sprinkle on some sea salt.

10 Leave to set in the fridge and make sure to share with your friends!

*Top tip!*
If you have any leftover melted chocolate, use it to make some hot chocolate. Heat up a mug full of milk with the leftover chocolate, a pinch of cinnamon and some extra cocoa powder, if it needs it, and enjoy!

## Easy swap

FRESH COFFEE OVER COFFEE PODS
Coffee pods are an environmental disaster, and have even been banned in some cities.[60]

# Sauces/Dips

### Tomato ketchup

I love to make my own homemade ketchup as it is quick to make and tastes so much better than any store-bought stuff.

INGREDIENTS

    2 tbsp tomato puree
    ½ tbsp sweetener *(maple syrup, brown sugar)*
    ¼ tsp garlic powder
    A dash of vinegar
    1 tbsp water
    Juice of ½ lemon
    ¼ tsp chilli flakes *(optional)*

METHOD

    Simply stir all the ingredients together.

## Easy swap

LOOSE FRUIT AND VEG
There are usually two options, one packaged,
one not, so pick the unpackaged!

# Pesto

Unfortunately, most pestos aren't vegan as they contain parmesan cheese (which is also not vegetarian either). But thankfully it's super easy to make at home! Pesto is of course perfect with pasta, but can be used in sandwiches, wraps, burgers, or as a dressing if thinned out with extra oil or water. Once you've made the pesto, store in a jar in the fridge for up to a week.

INGREDIENTS
> 2 garlic cloves, crushed
> Bunch of basil, trimmed
> 40g/1½ oz (⅓ cup) pine nuts or cashews
> Juice of 1 lemon
> 4 tbsp nutritional yeast
> Salt and pepper
> 2 tbsp olive oil

METHOD
> Blend the ingredients in a food processor until well mixed but still very textured, adding more oil if required.

*Top tip!*
> For some extra greens, try adding in a handful of spinach or kale to your pesto. Avocado, (thawed) peas or steamed broccoli also work really well!

## Easy swap

GLASS BOTTLES OVER PLASTIC BOTTLES
Peanut butter, ketchup, dressings and other
condiments can all be found in glass containers.

## Hummus

Who doesn't love hummus? It's certainly a staple for most vegans, and if you make it from scratch, you can avoid using the plastic tubs they usually come in from the shop. Simply blend the ingredients, taste, adding more of whatever you feel it needs, and enjoy!

INGREDIENTS

400g tin of chickpeas/125g dried chickpeas
1 tbsp tahini
Juice of 1 lemon
½ tsp cumin
½ tsp paprika
2 garlic cloves, crushed
4 tbsp water
2–3 tbsp olive oil
Salt and pepper
½–1 tsp chilli *(for some spice!) (optional)*

1   If using dried chickpeas, soak in water overnight. Drain the chickpeas and tip into a pan. Cover with cold water, bring to a boil and simmer for 45 minutes to an hour or until tender. Drain and rinse them ahead of making your hummus. If using tinned chickpeas then skip this step.

2   Tip the drained chickpeas into the food processor. Add the remaining ingredients and blend, taste, and adjust the seasoning.

### Easy swap

CARDBOARD OVER PLASTIC
Choose pastas, cereals, porridge and other foods packaged in cardboard rather than plastic.

# Salsa

If you haven't made fresh salsa before, please give this recipe a go, and you'll never buy the stuff from the shop again!

INGREDIENTS

4–6 large tomatoes, chopped
1 red onion, finely chopped
1 garlic clove, finely choped
1–2 chillies, deseeded and finely chopped
Bunch of coriander, chopped
Juice of 1 lemon or lime
Salt and pepper

METHOD

Mix the vegetables and herbs in a bowl with the lemon or lime juice. Season and serve! Keep refrigerated and use within a week.

# Drinks

## Hot chocolate

Homemade hot chocolate is a real treat that I like to make myself if I need something warming in the evenings. This recipe is truly a hug in a mug.

INGREDIENTS
Medium mug of plant milk
25g/1oz dark chocolate broken into chunks
½ tsp cinnamon
2 tsp cocoa powder

METHOD
1  Fill your favourite mug with the milk. Leave a little space at the top (for the chocolate).
2  Pour the milk into a pan with the remaining ingredients and stir over low to medium heat, making sure it doesn't come to a boil or overheat.
3  When the mixture is all melted and hot, pour back into your mug and enjoy!

# Smoothies

I love a good smoothie in the morning, and like so many of these recipes, they're so versatile and easily adaptable, with just a few key elements! Bananas work particularly well as a base to most smoothies to keep it filling, and from there I usually add one or two other fruits, a handful of greens, a dollop of nut butter or yoghurt, a combination of some add-ins such as chia seeds and protein powder, all topped off with my liquid of choice (which is usually some plant milk). Using the list below, pick one (or a few) from each to build your own smoothie!

FRUIT
*(try freezing for a creamier texture)*
Banana
Berries
Mango
Pineapple
Peach
Kiwi
Watermelon

GREENS
Kale
Spinach
Cucumber
Mint
Watercress
Celery

FAT/PROTEIN
Nut butters
Avocado
Coconut yoghurt
Coconut milk
Walnuts
Almonds

SUPPLEMENTS/ADD-INS
Green powder
Protein powder
Chia seeds
Flax seeds
Cacao/cocoa powder
Hemp seeds
Oats
Ginger
Cinnamon

LIQUID
Plant milk
Orange juice
Coconut water
Water

# six

—

# the home

# Decluttering Your Home

Minimalism and sustainability start at home: what you're cooking for dinner, the furniture that fills your rooms, how much stuff you hoard and the cleaning products you're using. I truly believe in the importance of having a home that is a sanctuary where you can unwind and relax, free from mess, disorganisation, clutter and unnecessary stuff. This can be achievable in so many ways in many different environments. Whether you have a tiny flat or bigger family home, it's about finding what works for you and what doesn't; what is serving a purpose and what isn't; what is hindering your eco habits and what is helping them. A few tweaks here and there can make a world of difference to how you experience your home, and the impact it has on your mindset and the environment. It's about going back to the essentials and simplifying the things that we really 'need' in our homes.

We use lots of energy at home, create lots of waste, and we hoard and hide lots of *stuff* – stuff we likely have forgotten about or just don't use anymore. If we get used to living simply at home, putting in place healthy habits and eco-friendly routines, we will set ourselves up for the outside world to continue these habits and routines. It all starts at home. After all, it's where we spend most of our time.

It's not about overhauling everything we do to make our lives more complicated (which it can sometimes feel like when changing routines and habits), but instead finding simpler and more sustainable ways to live. We can learn from our parents, our grandparents and our ancestors who lived sustainably in their communities and homes. For example, composting at first may seem like a complex and difficult thing to do. But it's a simple switch that can save lots of waste going to landfill, and instead puts it back in the earth. Similarly, decluttering and organising your home may seem like a big job you just don't have the time or energy for. But once you have simplified your living space and the things you own, you'll save time on cleaning and tidying every day. Not only that, but you're likely to enjoy the space you're in more now that it is clutter free!

Removing unnecessary stuff from around the home is the first and potentially most important step to minimising your space. The first chapter in this book delves deep into how to declutter your life, so let's once again revisit my step-by-step guide on how to declutter any area of your home. You might find that as you start to declutter, certain pieces of furniture or decorations no longer serve their purpose. You can therefore declutter these larger items to make more room around your home.

Consider items around your home that you're *expected* to own, based on what everyone else does, that you don't actually feel you need. Maybe you don't own enough clothes to fill a wardrobe *and* chest of drawers or dresser. So stick to just the one, or opt for a hanging rail instead. Or you rarely watch TV. So ditch the TV and make seating the centre of your living space. Maybe you don't particularly like excessive amounts of decor, or pictures on the wall. So keep it simple with just some plants and empty space on your walls. Ask yourself the following questions:

- Are there any pieces of furniture that take up too much space?
- Am I filling the room with items just for the sake of it? What would it look like without them?
- Are there surfaces filled with clutter that serve no purpose, functionally or aesthetically?

- Is the colour palette bringing the room down?
- Am I choosing this decor based on what is on trend, or what I personally like?

This is one of the most satisfying parts of minimising your home: putting everything in its place. A great way to organise and declutter is to consider whether something has a place in your home or not. If it doesn't, you either need to get rid of it or find a proper place for it to organise away! Not only will this make it easier to find everything around the house, but it will stop you from purchasing something you already own!

Don't forget to delve into the hidden spaces in our homes where things lurk. Dusty attics, cluttered garages and dark cupboards are for putting things away and closing the door. These are places we like to hide things and forget about them, so make sure to leave no space unturned. This also includes your children's things, or anything you own for your pets. Nothing should be left unturned.

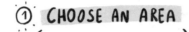

① CHOOSE AN AREA

## CATEGORY

FOOD AND DRINK
EQUIPMENT, APPLIANCES AND UTENSILS
BOOKS, PAPERS AND DOCUMENTS
ELECTRONICS
TOYS AND GAMES
FURNITURE AND DECOR
LINEN AND TOWELS
TOOLS AND OUTDOOR
SENTIMENTAL ITEMS

## AREA

BEDROOM
BATHROOM
LIVING ROOM
KITCHEN
DINING ROOM
OFFICE/STUDY
HALLWAY
CUPBOARD
LAUNDRY ROOM
ATTIC
GARAGE
BASEMENT
OUTDOOR SPACES

② TAKE EVERYTHING OUT

# Sustainable and Minimal Home Swaps

There are some really simple swaps we can make around the home in an effort to be more sustainable and reduce the things we own. Find a few that you could easily swap, and you can make a big difference to the waste you produce, energy you use and space taken up in your home. This doesn't mean you should throw out what you have and buy new sustainable versions, but if you run out or it reaches the end of its life, have a think about opting for a more sustainable option.

| BATHROOM | SWAP |
| --- | --- |
| Plastic toothbrush | Bamboo toothbrush |
| Plastic packaged toothpaste | Toothpowder/tooth tabs, toothpaste in a jar/aluminium tube |
| Plastic packaged soap, shower gel | Unpackaged multipurpose bar of soap, glass packaged soap/ shower gel, refillable bulk soap |
| Plastic packaged beauty products | See Chapter 3 for all of my tips and recipes on how to make your own and reduce on waste |
| Cotton pads, face wipes | Flannel, reusable bamboo/ cotton pads |
| Single-use tampons/sanitary towels | Reusable cloth pads, menstrual cup, period underwear, tampon applicator, compostable organic tampons |
| Disposable plastic razor | Safety razor |
| Plastic hairbrush/comb | Wooden hairbrush/comb |

| | |
|---|---|
| Toilet roll | Recycled toilet roll, paper packaged toilet roll, bidet/ bidet shower attachment |
| Plastic loofah | Natural loofah/natural bath brush |

See Chapter 3 for DIY beauty tips to further reduce waste in the bathroom.

| KITCHEN | SWAP |
|---|---|
| Paper towels | Dish towels/cloths, reusable/ compostable dish cloths |
| Plastic containers/Tupperware | Glass or aluminium jars and containers |
| All–purpose waste bin | Separate indoor compost bin, recycling bins and waste bin |
| Plastic bin bags | Compostable bin bags |
| Disposable wipes/ microfibre plastic cloths | Reusable natural fibre cloths (you can make your own by cutting up an old cotton T–shirt) |
| Plastic shopping bags | Reusable shopping bags, cloth/ mesh food produce bags |
| Plastic food packaging | Mason jars to store food in bulk |
| Cling film/aluminium foil | Reusable wax wrapping |
| Plastic straws | Reusable metal/glass/bamboo straws |

| | |
|---|---|
| Plastic utensils | Wooden or metal utensils |
| Plastic sponges | Reusable natural fibre cloths, biodegradable sponges, loofah, wooden brush, recycled plastic sponges |
| Plastic cutting board | Wooden cutting board |
| Parchment paper | Reusable silicone baking sheet |
| Paper napkins | Cloth napkins |
| Bottled water | Filtered tap water |
| Tea bags (most have plastic in their packaging) and coffee pods | Loose leaf tea with a tea strainer and ground coffee with cafetière or stovetop espresso maker/moka pot |
| Paper cupcake baking cases | Reusable silicone baking cases, silicone cupcake tray |
| Paper/plastic plates, paper/plastic cutlery | Reusable plates and cutlery |
| Plastic bags | Reusable silicone bags, reusable containers |
| Teflon pans | Cas-iron or stainles-steel pans |

| BEDROOMS AND LIVING SPACES | SWAP |
| --- | --- |
| Synthetic bed sheets | Cotton, bamboo or linen bedding (natural fibres) |
| New furniture | Vintage/secondhand/repurposed furniture |
| Classic lightbulbs | LED or energy saving lightbulbs |
| Radiators on full | Hot water bottle, radiators turned down low, draft excluders under doors |
| Tissues | Cloth handkerchief |
| Paraffin wax candles | Soy/coconut/rapeseed wax candles |
| Plug-in air freshener | Reed diffuser and essential oils |
| New CDs, DVDs, books, magazines | Secondhand CDs, DVDs and books, online subscriptions, streaming services |
| Cut flowers | Potted plants |
| Fabric conditioner | White vinegar, essential oils |
| Tumble dryer | Drying rack/clothes horse/outdoor clothes line |

# Minimalist Home Routines and Habits

All the clutter around our homes can cause a visual distraction, making the space less enjoyable to be in. Similarly, the more clutter, the more dust it will collect and the more things we need to keep cleaning. I just love the look and feel of my home being clutter-free, open and full of light and simplicity. Some of these habits help me to stay on top of my home being clean, organised and tidy, so see if they make yours less cluttered and more calm too!

1   CLEAN UP EVERY EVENING

Keeping a house in order can be time-consuming, especially with a busy life, children, families and lots of adult responsibilities. One of the best habits to develop to keep on top of things is to clean up every evening before bed. Do the dishes, fluff the pillows, put things away where they belong and give everything a quick wipe down. If you're not living alone get your family/partner/housemates to join in with the chores every day to make sure you're all contributing to a clutter-free home. Plus I find the routine quite therapeutic at the end of a long day!

2   DECLUTTER REGULARLY

I've been decluttering for years now, and honestly, it never ends. We receive gifts on our birthdays, holidays, when we achieve something or when we move home. We break some things, replace others, stop using stuff and are constantly consuming. Even as minimalists it's hard not to consume and bring new things into the home. So be mindful of staying on top of your clutter-free space by regularly decluttering things that may have started to build up, or that you no longer want or need in your home.

3   CLEAR SURFACES

One of the easiest ways to keep your home tidy and clutter-free is to get rid of the things piling up on the surfaces around you. The items on your kitchen counters – how many of these need

to be out on display? The decorations on your mantelpiece –
do you enjoy them, or are there a few too many? The random
things at the end of your kitchen table – can they be tidied away
elsewhere? Go around your home and find places for things that
are cluttering up surfaces and try minimising on the number of
decorations sitting around your home.

4 FIND PLACES FOR EVERYTHING

No more junk drawer, no more piles of letters and no more
random items that have no home. Declutter and find places for
every last item in your house. This not only makes it easier to
tidy things away as you know where everything belongs, but it
stops you from keeping things that you just don't need.

5 QUALITY OVER QUANTITY

Instead of filling your home with lots of things you have
collected over the years that you're not sure you like or use
anymore, choose to keep just the things you love. Similarly,
when buying new pieces for your home or redecorating, rather
than buying lots of cheap pieces to fill out a room that won't last
more than a year or two, consider spending a little more now on
a higher-quality timeless piece that will stand the test of time.

# How to Have an Eco-home

Now that we have a clutter-free space, let's make it as eco-friendly as possible! This doesn't require moving house, or installing expensive devices, just a few small changes that can make a big impact.

1  RENEWABLE ENERGY

Fossil fuels for energy need to be a thing of the past, and you can start by switching to using renewable energy in your home. It's no more expensive to switch to a green-energy provider, and they also offer the option to carbon offset your gas.

2  LED LIGHTBULBS

I've mentioned it before, but LED lightbulbs are so much more energy efficient than regular lightbulbs. Normal filament bulbs heat up to produce light, therefore using more energy than LED bulbs which don't need to do this. They are 80 per cent more efficient as 95 per cent of the energy in LEDs is converted into light, and only 5 per cent is wasted as heat. They also last a lot longer, requiring fewer replacements therefore fewer resources used overall.

3  RECHARGEABLE BATTERIES

Rather than replacing your batteries every time they run out, using rechargeable ones means that you can continuously use the same ones over and over again. It's a really easy swap that can make a big difference over time.

4  AIR–DRY LAUNDRY

Tumble-drying was always a luxury growing up, so air-drying in my home was the norm. I still don't own a tumble dryer and want to encourage you to give air-drying a go if you don't already. It will save you money on those expensive spins and reduce the overall energy usage of your home.

5   DRAUGHT EXCLUDERS

Keeping the warmth in can be difficult in some homes, so this is where draught excluders come in handy. If you have a sewing machine, try making one of your own by sewing a tube from fabric and filling it with wheat grain.

6   REPAIR AND REPURPOSE

When things break, don't simply throw them out and replace them with a newer version, but find ways in which you can repair or repurpose. Lots of furniture can be fixed with a lick of paint, new handles or a quick sand.

7   SECONDHAND FURNITURE AND APPLIANCES

Every time you want something new for your home, try to find it secondhand first. I know I'm a stuck record at this point, but if more of us did this we could make a significant difference. You'll save money, add character to your home, get creative with upcycling projects, all while reducing the resources needed to decorate.

8   GROW YOUR OWN VEG

From lettuce to potatoes, courgettes, carrots, onions and herbs, try growing different things that you use in the kitchen regularly. Even if you don't have a garden, you can create a herb garden or grow salad leaves or pea shoots on your windowsill!

9   SAVE ENERGY WHILE COOKING

Thinking about how you're cooking your food can save lots of energy. Keep lids on your saucepans to heat them faster, and defrost things overnight rather than in the microwave. Try using residual heat too. If you bring your pasta to a boil, for example, you can turn the heat down to let it simmer rather than having the heat up so high and continuously boiling.

10 SWITCHING OFF THE WATER

It can be easy to forget to consider how much water you're actually using. When showering, switch off the water when shaving your legs, for example. When washing up, plug and fill the sink rather than using a continuous stream. By simply being more mindful you can easily reduce your resources over time.

## Homemade cleaning products

Every time we go to the shops there is a new cleaning product on sale that we didn't know we needed. Most of these products have toxic and environmentally harmful ingredients and are packaged in lots of plastic. We're sold different cleaning products for every room, surface, fixture and fitting in our houses. But the reality is, you just don't need it all! Some harmful ingredients used in regular cleaning products can have adverse effects on our health, triggering asthma and allergies, irritating our skin or causing serious implications such as declining our lung health over time. Long-term use of lots of unnecessary cleaning sprays is something we should try to avoid, and instead we should switch to purchasing non-toxic cleaners and simplifying our cleaning routine to the basics.

Half the time a cloth and soapy water easily does the job, but there are also some basic ingredients that you can use alone or mix together for various cleaning purposes around the home. This will not only save money, but reduce plastic usage and lessen the environmental and household pollution caused by the manufacture, use and disposal of shop-bought cleaning products.

### BICARBONATE OF SODA/BAKING SODA

Bicarbonate of soda has been used for over a century as a way to deodorise, clean and scour away dirt. The soda will fizz up when mixed with liquid and cleanse away marks and stains. You can easily use this alone to clean sinks, toilets, baths, ovens, fridges and surfaces.

### CASTILE SOAP

One of the most versatile products you can buy, castile soap can be used as an all-purpose cleaner all around your home. From laundry detergent to dish soap, hand soap, floor cleaner and even shampoo, castile soap has got you covered. Remember that it's a concentrated liquid, so a little goes a long way. It's safe for allergies, if you have a skin condition such as eczema or psoriasis and around babies or pets.

### WHITE VINEGAR

Another incredible multi-purpose product, this can be used all over the home to get rid of stains, grease, dirt, odours, mould and mildew. It may have a slightly off-putting smell, but this quickly dissipates, or can be counteracted by delicious-smelling essential oils.

### LEMON JUICE

A very strong acid, the juice of a lemon helps to fight against bacteria, remove stains and keep your whites white, as it acts as a natural bleach. The smell is also lovely and refreshing!

### OLIVE OIL

Perfect for polishing furniture, olive oil is great at loosening up stains, grease and grime on all sorts of surfaces.

### ESSENTIAL OILS

Naturally anti-bacterial, essential oils not only help to sanitise your house, but keep it smelling great too. Some of the best to go for are lavender, tea tree and lemon.

### SALT

Salt is a versatile mineral that has a nifty way of scouring off dirt. It will also boost the cleaning effects of other ingredients, such as vinegar or bicarbonate of soda, when combined together.

### SOAP NUTS

These magical berries produce a natural soap called saponin that foams up and removes grime and smells when mixed with water. They're anti-fungal, anti-bacterial and anti-microbial, working as a great eco-friendly alternative to other toxic cleaners.

*Top tip!*

    Try to use up the cleaning products you already have first, then keep the bottles for when you make your own! See if a friend or even a local company can take the supplies you don't see yourself using.

# Easy Recipes for DIY Cleaning Products

## All-purpose cleaner

1 part white vinegar
1 part water
10 drops of essential oils

This all-purpose cleaner can be used all over the home to wipe
down surfaces, and sanitise it. You can also try infusing your
vinegar with the rind of lemons or oranges to offset the scent.
You can do this by adding citrus rinds to a jar, cover with white
vinegar, seal and store in a cupboard for 2–4 weeks. Once the
vinegar has infused, strain and use alongside normal vinegar in
this mixture to add a fresh scent (this is a concentrated liquid
so you don't need much of it to get a nice smell). Avoid use on
marble, stone or granite surfaces.

## Toilet cleaner

1 part white vinegar
Bicarbonate of soda
10 drops of your favourite essential oil

For a sparkling loo, glug in some white vinegar, a good shake
of bicarbonate of soda with around 10 drops of your favourite
essential oil into the basin. Leave to sit for a few minutes, scrub
with the toilet brush, fizzing up the mixture and getting rid
of all the nasties. Use the above all-purpose cleaner for the
surfaces of the toilet, leaving to sit for a minute or two before
wiping away.

## Laundry detergent

Homemade soap nut laundry liquid.

15–20 soap nuts
2 litres/3½ pints water

Simply add the soap nuts to the water in a pan and bring to
a boil. Allow to cool with a lid on and then strain into a jar
or bottle. Add 250ml/9oz (1 cup) (double this for a large or
particularly dirty load) of this liquid in the drawer of your
washing machine. Store the liquid in the fridge.

You can also add 5–7 soap nuts into your washing machine
in a muslin washbag (they usually come with these when you
buy them). You can reuse the soapnut pouch for around four
to five washes, until they turn grey. And the coolest thing is
that when you're done with them, they can be composted in
your garden!

## Windows and mirrors

1 part white vinegar
4 parts water
10 drops of lemon essential oil

Use this diluted mixture on your windows to leave them
polished and clean. My favourite essential oil to use for
this is lemon. Try to avoid doing this on a hot day as it can
leave streaks.

## Air freshener

10+ drops of essential oil
Spray bottle of water

Add the essential oil to the water, give the mixture a sniff and a
spray, and add a few more drops of oil if it needs it. Go slowly:
less is more when it comes to essential oils! When you're happy
with the scent, then you can use it to freshen up the air, your
furniture or linen. Fresh scents such as lavender work really well
for air freshener.

## Mould and mildew

Spray bottle of white vinegar
6–8 drops of tea tree oil

Spritz the affected area and let it sit for around 30 minutes.
Rinse off with warm water and scrub off with a cloth if it needs
some assistance!

## Microwave cleaner

Place a small cup of vinegar and the juice of a lemon in the
microwave and switch it on for 2 minutes. Leave the door
closed for a further minute or so to steam, then open and
simply wipe down the inside with a damp cloth. No need to
awkwardly scrub!

## Washing-up liquid/dish soap

Castile soap works perfectly as a washing-up liquid as well!
Simply mix 4 parts castile soap to 1 part water in a repurposed
container of your choice and use on your dishes.

## Furniture polish

¼ cup white vinegar
¾ cup olive oil *(choose the cheap option rather than extra virgin)*
Juice of ½ lemon

Olive oil is a really effective furniture polish as it will protect
wood from scratches and rings. Combine all the ingredients,
then apply with a soft cloth and rub in a circular motion across
the surface of the furniture, particularly in any problem areas.

## Floor cleaner

Bucket of hot water
¼ cup white vinegar
A squeeze of castile soap *(a little goes a long way)*

Fill up your bucket of hot water and add the vinegar and castile
soap. Scrub the floors using this mixture with a mop or cloth
and be left with shiny surfaces! The vinegar will polish and clean
as the castile soap helps to get rid of any dirt.

## Carpet deodoriser

Jar of bicarbonate of soda *(leave a little space for shaking)*
10 drops of essential oil

Shake together and store for use on carpets when they need
freshening up. All you need to do is shake over your carpet, leave
for up to 30 minutes and then vacuum. Your carpets should
smell really lovely and fresh.

## Oven cleaner

¼ cup bicarbonate of soda
1 tsp salt
A dash of water

In a small bowl, add the soda and salt and then keep adding water bit by bit until you create a paste. Cover your oven in the mixture and let it sit overnight. Scrub and wipe clean the next day with a damp cloth, and voila, sparkling oven!

## Chopping board cleaner

To disinfect your chopping boards, chop a lemon in half and rub over the surface of your chopping board, then wipe clean. If you have any tough stains, then you can squeeze some of the lemon juice onto the chopping board and let it sit for a few minutes before wiping it off.

## Drain cleaner

For a blocked drain, pour a good amount of bicarbonate of soda followed by some white vinegar into your drain. These two ingredients will react together to break down any dirt, grime and grease clogging up the drain. After 10–15 minutes, pour boiling-hot water down the drain to clean everything out (make sure to only do this on metal pipes, as the boiling water could melt the plastic pipes – otherwise just turn on the hot water tap).

## Stain remover

¼ cup white vinegar
¼ cup bicarbonate soda
A squeeze of castile soap
2 cups water

Mix, shake and store in a spray bottle to use whenever you have a tough stain on your clothes or the carpet. Shake before use each time.

## Easy swaps

Use what you already have, but if you need
a new one, make it more sustainable!

PLASTIC DISH BRUSH OVER WOODEN DISH
BRUSH WITH PLANT-BASED BRISTLES

PLASTIC SCOURER OVER A LOOFAH

MICROFIBRE CLOTHS OVER COTTON CLOTHES
/SCRAP CLOTHS

PLASTIC TOILET BRUSH OVER WOODEN TOILET BRUSH

# Easy Home DIY

There are so many ways we can upcycle or restore things to save us replacing and buying something new. So before you get rid of that piece of furniture for a new one, see if there is a way you can fix it up to restore it to its former glory. Get creative and make it a fun project to make something with your hands!

1   FURNITURE UPCYLING

A coat of paint can do so much to an old or stained piece of furniture. Prep your furniture by lightly sanding the wood and protecting any handles or details with masking tape. Brush on thin layers of paint, allowing time to dry in between, until fully covered. If you are going for a rustic look, add equal parts water to your chosen paint and brush on thin layers until you've reached the desired opacity. You can also sand corners and edges of the furniture to give it that worn-in feel. New handles to a chest of drawers or cupboard can be the perfect finishing touch to your project.

2   KITCHEN MAKEOVER

Give your kitchen a new lease of life with a few touches! This could mean simply painting the cabinets, or applying new covers to the doors. New handles can also make a big difference to an older kitchen. Reclaimed wood can make a feature shelf to store some of your favourite jars, bowls and plates. Find new storage solutions to keep things neat, and free up space. You can even buy tile paint to cover any old-fashioned designs.

3   JARS JARS JARS

Jars are one of my favourite things to reuse around the home. Aside from storing food they can be used to hold pens, pencils, makeup brushes, kitchen utensils, candles, as a vase or plant pot. You could also try attaching rope and hanging them outside with tea lights, or inside with some plants (a windowsill herb garden would be perfect). To get a tough sticker off, use a little oil and/or some boiling water.

4  WOODEN PALLETS

Wooden pallets can be used to make a variety of different pieces of furniture around your home, and can be found in so many places, including building merchants, warehouses and local shops. Have a look around your town and see if you can spot any and pop in to ask if they're available. They can be sanded, painted or stained and securely screwed together to make really cool outdoor seating or a bed. Just top with some comfy cushions or a mattress. You could also turn them into a garden planter or table!

5  TIN CANS

Tin cans, like jars, can be used for so many purposes other than storing food. I use tin cans as pen holders, to make my own candles or you can use one as a simple plant pot. You can also paint or cover them with fun paper to make them stand out. A fun way is to dip just the bottom half into paint!

6  REPURPOSING CLOTHES

Old clothes can be made into other things for your home after you've made the decision to declutter them. Cosy jumpers can be used as cushion covers simply by measuring to fit the cushion, cutting, sewing together and either adding some buttons or making into an envelope cushion. Any clothes that are stained or ripped can be cut up to form rags and cloths for cleaning.

# A Tidy Home

Now that you've decluttered, organisation is key to keeping your space neat and tidy. With less stuff, organisation becomes a lot easier. It's important to make sure everything in your house has a home.

- Use cardboard boxes or repurposed containers to store jewellery, electronics or makeup in your drawers.
- Colour coordinate your clothes or books.
- Find hidden storage solutions for unattractive items on display, such as under the bed storage, or wicker baskets.
- Find a place for everything. No junk drawers, and no piles of stuff at the end of your kitchen table.
- Keep decluttering as things come in. It isn't a one-time thing, but a consistent effort to keep the home clutter free.
- Opt for neutral tones, natural textures and materials to create a calm and tidy feel. Lots of textures and colours can become overwhelming and busy.
- Owning less decor means less fluffing of pillows in the evening, less dusting of ornaments, and less putting things away.
- Create a cleaning routine once a week to tidy everything in your home. Get your family or roommates involved to make it a group effort.

# Decorating a Minimal Home

The next big step is to do a little redecorating. Whether you're taking away, adding or moving stuff around, changing up the space once you've decluttered and organised can be the final touch to minimising your space.

Minimalism is less about aesthetics and more about a mindset and how things feel. So while you can decorate in a minimalist aesthetic, you don't have to. What you can do is create a space that is clutter-free and calming. Just reduce, minimise and simplify where it makes sense in your home. If a space is decluttered but still colourful, for example, this is using minimalism to your own standards in your own home. There is no use in redecorating your home in all white and getting rid of things that make you happy, just for the sake of attaining that 'minimalist' look. You do you.

Try some of the ideas below to achieve a minimalist space:

- Add plants instead of lots of nick-nacks to add some colour and life into a room without being cluttered. Plus they'll purify and clean the air.
- Stick to a colour and style theme throughout your home to achieve a flow throughout the different spaces.
- Choose your furniture carefully for a purpose, and to fit a space. This will help the flow of your home and avoid it feeling busy.
- Find your happy medium between owning what you love and keeping a clutter-free space.
- If you love particular colours, use them on accent walls and in decorations such as rugs or pillows.
- Any collections of things that you enjoy, such as books, art supplies or electronics (any collections, hobbies or work items), can become a feature in a room if you take time to organise their display.

# Guide to Composting

Why do we need to compost? Doesn't waste compost in landfill anyway?

Unfortunately not. Air can't get to the organic waste once it's piled up in landfill, and therefore when it breaks down it creates methane, a harmful greenhouse gas. However, if we compost at home, air is able to reach the waste and it decomposes anaerobically, meaning very little methane is produced. The resulting compost can be used as fertiliser for your garden (your plants will love it as it will be full of nutrients and microorganisms to help them grow).

Essentially you're using up this valuable resource rather than throwing it away. Not only are you stopping a huge heap of waste going to landfill, but you're also reducing the costs and impact of waste collection and putting this waste into nourishing the earth. A beautiful and complete cycle!

Compost helps to maintain soil quality and fertility. It is a mild natural fertiliser, and therefore a much better option than chemical fertiliser that can end up in our rivers and streams. It helps the soil to retain water, keeping it moisturised and it provides the plants with everything they need to grow big and strong. It's a really huge sustainability lifestyle step that more of us need to be doing to prevent air pollution, reduce waste and return nutrients to the earth. Plus your bin will be a whole heap lighter!

## Garden composting

The best way to compost is of course in your own garden. You can simply create a pile of some of your vegetable scraps, dead leaves or grass clippings, but most likely you'll want a bin to keep it contained.

Make sure to place the bin on bare soil as this will help it to aerate and enable insects to get to it. You can also place your compost bin on paving, decking or concrete, but be aware that the bin will stain these surfaces and you just need to add some soil to the bottom of the bin.

*Top tips!*

- It's important that you compost a mixture of dry (leaves, cardboard boxes) and wet things (food scraps, grass cuttings) to get the right mixture of carbon and nitrogen in your mixture.
- Try to break everything up (where possible) before adding to your compost bin to help it to break down faster. For example, if you're adding cardboard, cut this up into smaller pieces before adding to your bin.
- Turn your compost regularly to aerate it, helping things to decompose faster. You want to get the right balance in your compost so it isn't too dry or wet. If it is getting wet then it needs turning, and if it is dry hose it down. Feed *and* water those microorganisms.
- Know what can or can't go in your compost bin. I've listed the dos and don'ts of composting on the next page.
- Knowing when your compost is ready to use is also important. It will become a near-black soil at the base of your bin which will be rich with nutrients. You can use this soil across your flowerbeds and vegetable patches to improve the soil quality, help retain moisture and suppress weeds. And no more need for chemical fertilisers or pesticides.

| YES | NO |
| --- | --- |
| Vegetable food scraps (stalk, leaves, peel and all) | Animal products (dairy, meat, fish, bones) |
| Cut flowers | Non-vegetarian manure (dogs, cats) |
| House plants | Cigarette ends |
| Garden plants and debris | Cooking oils |
| Hedge clippings | Coated or coloured paper |
| Grass clippings | Weeds |
| Leaves | Diseased garden waste |
| Tea leaves and bags (make sure they don't contain plastic, as many do) | |
| Coffee grounds | |
| Hay and straw | |
| Cardboard | |
| Black and white newspaper | |
| Printed paper | |
| Wood shavings/sawdust | |
| Vegetarian animal manure (cows, horses, rabbits, hamster) | |

## Apartment composting

I didn't always have a garden when composting, so had to find ways around it to put my food waste back into the earth. Here are a few different ways you can still compost while living in an apartment or without a garden.

1 FOOD WASTE COLLECTION

Find out if food waste can be collected from your door along with the rest of your rubbish and recycling. This isn't available in all areas, but is worth finding out from your local council.

2   WORM BINS/WORMERY

Worm bins are an easy way to compost indoors by using the power of worms to break down your food. They need to be kept in warm, moist conditions, so a utility room, kitchen or balcony would be ideal. You can either buy a worm bin or create your own by following tutorials found online.

3   BOKASHI SYSTEM

The bokashi system uses a large bucket that you add your compost to, mash it down, then add an activator mix full of microbes that will speed up the decomposition of the waste.

4   LOCAL COMMUNITY GARDEN

This is the option I went for when living without a garden. It was as easy as calling up my local council and being directed to local community gardens that accepted food scraps for their compost bins. We collected our waste in a small bin inside, emptying it into a larger one outside when it became full, and then took it to the local garden every two or three weeks. A great and simple way to keep your local community garden alive!

5   FARMERS' MARKET

Farmers sometimes have compost piles that they are happy for you to donate to. So next time you're at the farmers' market, find out if there is someone who is keen to take your waste and make it into a useful resource for their farm.

6   ASK AROUND

If all else fails, ask around! You might have neighbours who are avid gardeners who would love to take your food waste off your hands to use for their compost, or maybe someone has chickens that they'd feed your scraps to. Maybe there is another avid environmentalist at your office, kid's school or on your street. Explore every avenue to find out if someone will be happy to take it off your hands, I know I would!

# seven

—

# travel

# My Travel Experience

In the past I've flown a lot: around southeast Asia, across the ocean to Canada and all over Europe. As someone who is so afraid of flying, I've often wondered where I caught the travel bug from. I flat out refused to get on a plane when I was a kid because I was so terrified of the idea of it. But then I started hearing about the amazing experiences my friends had during their gap year, and started wanting what I was seeing online. YouTubers, Instagrammers and bloggers were in a new country every time they posted, surrounded by blue water and seemingly living the dream life of being on a permanent holiday. I wanted to do what they were doing, so I got on that plane and started to explore.

During these travel experiences I've learnt a lot. I've had some of the best times of my life. But I've also realised that travel is as much life-changing and exciting as it is disappointing and tiring. While trying new cuisines and soaking up a different culture is wonderful, so is sitting at home in your dressing gown with a cuppa. I love to travel, but I also love being at home. There is an element of expectation and stress that comes with traveling so far from home that I don't think is discussed often enough. So I wanted to put it out there that I feel it too. Slowing things down, assessing what suits you in terms of travel, and being more mindful as you do so are all important.

This means minimising your expectations. Instead of lusting after a highlight reel from social media, understand what you want out of travel (or whether you want it at all). The girl in a bikini perfectly posed against the bluest of blue sea may be totally homesick. Travel can be as un-glam as hopping on a train to a town you've never been to before, or going camping with friends an hour or two away in the countryside. It doesn't have to cost the earth, nor does it have to damage the Earth.

Another element of travel that I've learnt over the years is how to do it more mindfully and sustainably. I used to over-pack every time I went on holiday, taking a huge suitcase full of different outfits for every day, and items for every eventuality. I couldn't understand how my friends managed with just carry-on luggage! I also wouldn't think much about the resources used to get me to where I was going, nor plan ahead in order to avoid using single-use plastic. But I've learnt about new ways to travel that aren't as polluting, how to downsize my luggage and plan ahead by bringing reuseables. A few simple tweaks can make a dramatic difference to your impact as you travel.

## Travel's Damaging Impact

Now let's get the elephant in the room out of the way. There is increasing discussion surrounding flying in particular, and the huge amounts of harmful emissions such as carbon dioxide and nitrogen oxide it produces. Around the world, flying emits about 860 million metric tons of carbon dioxide every year, or about 2 per cent of total global greenhouse gas emissions[61], while tourism in general accounts for around 8 per cent of global greenhouse gas emissions[62]. Not only that, but the polluting happens high in the atmosphere where the emissions can do more damage. While planes are comparable to cars in their fuel consumption per passenger mile, it's the huge distances that they can cover so easily that causes a big problem for our planet.

The amount people around the world are flying has significantly shot up since the 1970s and more of us are taking longer flights to explore new realms we've never seen before. Flying has become the fastest-growing cause of climate change in recent years, partially due to the increasingly cheap prices (as a result of low tax on air travel). Budget airlines are making it easier for people to fly further than they used to. While this exploration of the world via planes can be seen as positive – we get to experience different cultures to our own, take time away from our stressful jobs or be with our friends and family who are far from us – it doesn't come without a cost.

This is definitely one of the areas I've had to think more about recently on my journey towards being more sustainable. It can be a tough pill to swallow to understand how harmful flying around the world is – especially when there are so many places you still want to visit. But I think it's important that we all consider how much we fly, what for, and whether we can find alternative methods of travel.

| RETURN FLIGHTS | $CO_2$ |
|---|---|
| London–Paris (432.15 miles) | 0.11 tonnes |
| London–New York (6,884 miles) | 1.5 tonnes |
| London–Bali (via Dubai) (16,142.68 miles) | 3.56 tonnes |
| London–Sydney (via Dubai) (21,800 miles) | 4.81 tonnes |
| NYC–LA (4,914 miles) | 1.08 tonnes |
| LA–Sydney (14,988 miles) | 3.31 tonnes |

# Calculate your trip!

Eurostar London–Paris cuts CO2 emissions
per passenger by 90 per cent.[63]

| LONDON–PARIS (1 PASSENGER) | TRAIN | CAR | PLANE |
|---|---|---|---|
| **Carbon dioxide** (in kg) | 14.9 | 72.6 | 122.1 |
| **Energy resource consumption** (litre gasoline equivalent) | 14.4 | 32.3 | 51.9 |
| **Particulate matter** (in g) | 4.6 | 7.1 | 10.6 |
| **Nixtrogen oxides** | 39.4 | 301.2 | 497.9 |

www.climatecare.org/calculator
www.carbonfootprint.com/calculator.aspx
www.ecopassenger.org

The good thing is that there is a solution: flying less. If we are lucky enough to be of the 2–3 per cent of the world's population who flies internationally every year, we must take responsibility for its impact. The negative results of flying will affect a much larger and poorer population than those of us who have the luxury to fly for leisure. Finding different options that don't have quite the same impact, but will still offer the same elements of fun, adventure and friendship, is what we should all aim towards. If there is an easy alternative for you to travel – take the train or other mode of transport – on your next trip, then this is where you can start making a big change.

It can be frustrating that planes are often the cheapest and easiest option to get somewhere. I think by this point we're noticing a trend that convenience can come at a lesser cost to our wallets, but a greater cost to the environment. You're likely to only have a certain budget for your yearly trip away, as well as a set amount of time. You don't necessarily want to use the few days you have booked off from work travelling long distances on trains. I totally get it.

**But where there's a will there's a way:**

- Let's make public transport and trains cool! When making your travel plans, look into whether you can get there while avoiding getting on a plane.
- Instead of flying abroad, get a train somewhere in your own country you've never been to before (think of tourists from all over the world who visit places close to you that you take for granted).
- Make the train a part of your holiday by travelling somewhere slowly and stopping off at multiple locations as you go. The journey will show you beautiful sights along the way too that you'd miss on a plane.
- If you do travel by plane, make it a shorter distance rather than a long-haul flight.
- Instead of flying every year on holiday, change to flying every *other* year.
- Carbon offset your flight. Go online and find a reputable organisation that calculates the CO2 impact of your flight, and offers climate positive causes that you can contribute money towards to counteract your travel emissions. www.carbonfootprint.com
- If you have to fly, incorporate public transport into your trip by getting a train or bus to and from the airport at both ends.
- Buses are a great option (I once got a bus from London to Brussels) and are usually very cheap.
- If you're UK-based and visiting nearby countries, such as France or Belgium, getting the Eurostar is an easy option that gets you to Europe very fast at an affordable price.

It's inevitable that when we travel we have a larger impact and use more resources than we would at home – and in just the space of a few years, travelling abroad has gone from a once-a-year luxury to something more of us are doing spontaneously and regularly. We're using energy and fuel to get somewhere new and often consuming a lot more than we would ordinarily in our day-to-day lives. But there are some easy things you can do to travel in a more eco-friendly way and prepare yourself ahead of time. A lot of this involves forming new habits, being mindful and simply thinking ahead.

# How to Avoid Overtourism

It's no surprise that tourism, one of the world's biggest industries, has a hugely damaging impact on the environment and the residents of a country. Overtourism means that local residents are pushed out in favour of holiday homes, areas of beauty are constantly crowded, people consume more and consequently litter the environment. The affordability of cheap flights and accommodation services like Airbnb allow us to go on more holidays and visit more places, without much thought of the negative impact this will have on the places we're visiting. Yes, tourism can boost the local economy and create jobs, but this reliance on tourism can cause greater issues long term. So let's talk about how we can stop being a part of the problem.

- **Go somewhere that isn't full of tourists.** Instead of immediately visiting somewhere that everyone goes and you see posted all over social media, try to find a location where overtourism isn't an issue. It's likely to be just as beautiful and interesting, plus you'll avoid all the annoying crowds! Many places around the world have had to be closed off from tourists, due to their unsustainable actions and damage to the delicate environment.
- **Make your trip last and stay there longer.** Slow travel enables you to take your time to visit sites at your leisure, during less busy periods, and not have to cram everything into one weekend. Read more about slow travel at the end of this chapter.

- **Travel off-peak.** Where possible, save money and crowds by going during seasons when there will be fewer people. If we all gave this a go, maybe we'd be able to avoid the huge influx of people heading to places dealing with overtourism.
- **Travel independently and locally.** Don't rely on tour companies to take care of everything (oh, hi cruise ships), as this may mean your money isn't supporting the local economy. Find a local guide, and spend your money on local goods.
- **Do your research.** Think of what you want to see, do and experience during your time away to save wasting time. If you're better equipped, you can go about your holiday with less interference to the local community.
- **Go where you want to go.** Not only will it be a more meaningful trip, but you won't be following the crowd. Even though everyone and their mother seems to have gone to a particular place, it may not be for you.
- **Stay in a hotel in the centre.** If you can afford this, you'll avoid taking up space on public transport and stay in an area meant for tourists. Holiday lets, while cheap and useful, cause issues for locals by taking away long-term accommodation and enabling more and more people to visit their country without any form of regulation.
- **Find hidden gems.** While we all want to see the main tourist sites, sometimes there are places just as beautiful, but far less crowded.
- **Respect the locals.** You might be doing it for the gram, but is crowding in areas where people live, and queueing to get the shot really worth it? Aim to be invisible, and always be respectful.
- **Respect the culture.** Learn key phrases in the language, listen and learn about how people live, and don't expect it to be the same as it is at home.
- **Respect animals.** Animals all over the world are exploited in the name of tourism. Donkeys carrying people's luggage, elephant rides and photos with tigers. Don't fall for these 'attractions', but instead visit a sanctuary, or see animals in the wild.

# How to Travel Sustainably

## Reusables

Making sure you're armed with reusables on your trip will considerably reduce the amount of single-use plastic you will have to use on your travels.

### WATER BOTTLE

I will not leave my house without a reusable water bottle. Airports, train stations and cities often have water stations, but if not, just ask someone at a cafe or restaurant to refill your bottle.

Some countries might not have water that is safe for drinking (make sure to do your research beforehand), and if that's the case, I go to the supermarket and buy the biggest bottle of water I can carry. That way I can fill my bottle up each day and avoid having to buy smaller single-use water bottles when out and about. You can also buy water bottles that have built-in filters to make any tap water safe to drink!

### BAG

A canvas tote bag that can fold up in your luggage or backpack is ideal. Keep it in your backpack or handbag every day (it doesn't take up much room at all) so whatever you buy or use throughout the day, you'll have something to put it in! I often use it as my bag for food and water when travelling too, just to make it that little bit easier to access.

### TUPPERWARE

This can be an old plastic container, or a stainless-steel Tupperware that you've bought for this purpose. Having some form of food container will definitely come in handy when travelling. You may want to make your own lunch or snack for the travel day, and then you can use it during the remainder of your trip. I just ask nicely at any food stall or takeaway I go to if they can use my container to avoid it being served in plastic packaging. I've never had someone say no to this request, so don't be afraid to just ask if you're eating something on the go.

## CUTLERY

As with the Tupperware, having reusable cutlery means you
don't have to use the single-use plastic forks and spoons (or even
compostable ones – these are better than plastic but still don't beat
a reusable) that will be offered to you on trains, planes and when
ordering from food stalls on your holiday.
I have a really great lightweight wooden set that comes in a little
pouch to keep it all neat and tidy in my bag. But if you don't have
a set, you can easily just bring your own metal cutlery from home,
and wrap it up in a cloth napkin! You could also throw a reusable
straw in there if you think you'll want one during your time away.

## NAPKIN/HANDKERCHIEF

Which brings me to the napkin! I don't always bring one of these,
but they can be super useful if you regularly use tissues/napkins
when out and about. They're easy to throw in the wash and take up
no room at all.

## COFFEE CUP

Incredibly, 2,500,000,000 coffee cups are used every year in the
UK.[64] Having your own reusable cup means you can drink endless
cups of coffee and tea on the go without having to throw away any
single-use coffee cups. You can ask to use this on the train, a plane
or at a cafe during your trip. Many places in the UK even offer
discounts if you bring your own cup, which is a great initiative to
get more people to bring their own.

## BUY SMART

When we're away, with what feels like Monopoly money in hand,
we can quickly get spendy. We forget the rules we set for ourselves
at home when it comes to our budget; we want to get something
for our family and friends back home and we also want a memento
of our trip by bringing something back with us. Over the years I've
applied lots of the lessons I've learnt through minimalism when I
travel to reduce my spending habits and be more mindful about
shopping smart while away.

✳

## Shopping smart questions and checklist

Think of these questions when buying something abroad,
so you don't make a purchase you later regret:

○  Would I buy this if I was at home?

○  Can I easily bring this back home with me in my luggage?

○  Am I buying this gift for someone because I truly believe they
    would love it, or because I feel obligated to bring them back
    something?

○  Is this item overpriced for tourists?

○  Do I know where this product was made, and if the materials are
    sustainable?

○  Will I use this item, or is it something that will end up in a drawer
    somewhere never to be used?

Set yourself a budget for spending ahead of your trip so you
don't go overboard, or maybe tell yourself you'll only buy one
new item when away.

### Staycation

Instead of flying somewhere abroad, discover your own country! Not only will you avoid flying, but you are more likely to
live in a similar way to how you do day-to-day, therefore using
fewer resources. You'll know the shops, the language and the
things available to you, so are less likely to start getting carried
away. It's easy to take for granted what we have around us when
we live somewhere. But you'd be surprised what exciting and
new things you can find just around the corner from you.

## Go local

Whether you're abroad or in your own country on a trip, do your best to shop local. I love hunting out independent coffee shops, restaurants and market stalls when travelling to support the local economy, rather than going to chain restaurants or shops that I'm maybe more familiar with. It continues the same mindset that I have back home of shopping locally and ethically, and giving money to smaller local businesses.

## Eco accommodation

Do some research to find out if there are any eco accommodation options for your travels. There are more and more eco resorts, hotels and villas popping up nowadays that pride themselves on using renewable energy, reducing their waste and plastic usage, and filling their accommodation with sustainable products.

### HOSTELS

Probably the cheapest option for you to go for, but another eco-friendly alternative. As lots of people will be staying at one hostel, it's using the space resourcefully by sharing. Not only this, but you're likely to make some friends along the way!

### ECO HOTELS/RESORTS/VILLAS

Not all hotels or resorts are wasteful. There are some out there that make an effort to source everything sustainably, are careful about the waste they're producing in the kitchen and in their rooms, and run everything off renewable energy. Decisions have been made carefully to ensure their impact is lowered, so that you can lower your impact while travelling too!

### SELF-CATERED ACCOMMODATION

Opting to stay in self-catered accommodation that offers you all the facilities that you would have at home will always make it easier for you to travel sustainably and as waste-free as possible. Having the access to a full kitchen, and other facilities such as recycling bins, will enable you to avoid eating out as much while away (and therefore using plastic or creating food waste), and avoid the extras that come with hotels (think of all the small shampoo bottles, bed sheet changes, food waste from buffet breakfast).

SUN CREAM

Rather than picking up whatever sun cream you can find for your next holiday, source reef-friendly and cruelty-free sun protection. There are chemicals in lots of sunscreen, such as oxybenzone and octinoxate, that are particularly harmful to the ocean and coral reefs, and that we should therefore aim to avoid.

Look for oxybenzone-free sunscreens, ones with non-nano mineral zinc oxide, water resistance (so that less washes off your face and body into the ocean), paraben-free and labels that say 'reef safe/friendly' or 'coral safe/friendly'.

Similarly, do your research to make sure the brand isn't testing on animals or using animal products in their ingredient list.

## Clean up

A final sustainable plan of action is to pick up any litter you see when on your travels. This can be a specific effort one day to do a beach clean, or just a habit you implement whenever you're out and about. I like to think that when I go somewhere I am doing my bit to take care of the community in whatever way I can. Picking up after ourselves is so important, and by cleaning up litter you're stopping it from ending up in the wrong place or potentially harming wildlife.

# Minimalist Packing List

Now: what to pack?

Packing less and packing smart can save so much stress while travelling. Not only will you have less stuff you don't need to carry physically, but it overall becomes so much less of a burden while you're away. Spending less time worrying about what to wear, a quicker morning routine and a sense of living with less can be very satisfying.

I've put together a general list of things I might bring on a trip away with me. This would work for a five-day trip, or even a month-long trip. I find the only difference when it comes to what I pack for my travels is maybe one or two extra dresses or tops for variety, but everything else stays the same. I definitely wouldn't need all of this for a weekend away, so just use this as a general guide to help if you struggle to keep things to a minimum, or you know you'll be hopping from place to place.

It might seem like a long list when written out, but this will easily fit in either an average-sized backpack and carry-on suitcase, or a larger travel backpack (with maybe a tote bag/ small handbag for essentials so you can have them to hand).

## Travel outfit

I always wear something comfy for my travels, that also saves on space in my luggage. It usually consists of a pair of jeans or leggings, a plain T-shirt that I can wash and re-wear while I'm away, a sweater/jumper and a jacket/coat. Depending on how long I am away for, I will often wash this outfit and wear on the return home.

- Leggings/jeans
- Plain T-shirt
- Jumper/sweater
- Underwear/bra
- Socks
- Trainers/comfy shoes
- Jacket

## Backpack

Packing a backpack with your essentials makes everything a lot easier to access when on the go. It also means I'm prepared to avoid plastic! I'll wear this on the journey to keep everything to hand. I usually opt for a backpack over a handbag, as it is so much comfier to wear on long days exploring a new place!

- Reusable tote bag
- Reusable cutlery
- Reusable cup
- Reusable water bottle
- Wallet
- Keys
- Pen (and a notepad if you like writing)
- Portable charger/powerbank
- Phone
- Headphones
- Book/kindle
- Paracetamol/ibuprofen
- Laptop (and charger)
- Food/snacks (helps if you store this in a container too so you can wash and use this while you're away)
- Passport/travel tickets
- Essential toiletries (e.g. lip balm, moisturiser – omit from toiletries list if packing in your hand luggage)

## Clothes/shoes

- Pyjama top
- Pyjama bottoms
- 5 pairs underwear
- 2 bras
- 5 pairs of socks
- 2–4 dresses/dungarees/ playsuit/skirt (opt for two different styles/lengths for different purposes but make them comfy and easy to throw on)
- 1 pair of shorts
- 1 pair of trousers/jeans (depending on what you wore on the plane, bring another pair of bottoms)
- 2–4 tops (again, opt for different styles for different occasions such as a short sleeve vest, a blouse or a nicer evening top)
- 1–2 pairs of shoes (I'd opt for a smarter pair, and/or a weather-appropriate pair such as boots or sandals)
- 1–2 sets of workout clothing (again depending on where you're going and if you think you'll be exercising but I generally take this anyway just in case an activity pops up)
- Cross-body bag

## Toiletries

- Facial cleanser
- Moisturiser/facial oil
- Sunscreen (opt for cruelty free and coral friendly)
- Soap bar
- 2-in-1 shampoo/conditioner
- Deodorant
- Lip balm
- Toothbrush and toothpaste
- Hairbrush
- Menstrual cup/reusable sanitary towels
- Flannel
- Razor
- Hair product (I usually bring some argan oil to de-frizz)

## Makeup (if applicable)

- Light foundation/BB cream
- Concealer
- Mascara
- Cream blusher/bronzer
- Favourite lipstick (maybe a red lippy for the evenings or to dress up an outfit)
- Eyeliner

## Miscellaneous

- Sunglasses
- Medication (I always bring paracetamol/ibuprofen and some plasters/Band-Aids)
- Chargers
- Universal adapter plug
- Camera (with memory card)
- Small mirror

## Weather-depending additions

- 1–3 bikinis/swimsuits
- An extra jumper/sweater
- Waterproof jacket
- Beach towel
- Scarf/gloves/hat

# Slow Travel

In a world of fast food and same-day delivery, it can be difficult to slow down. But one of the amazing benefits of travel is that it can be a great opportunity to simplify things and slow the pace. You only have a backpack or suitcase of your belongings, you're taken away from your usual surroundings and habits and you (usually) aren't working; you're just living, breathing and taking in the world.

Travelling slowly and getting to know the local people and culture has become my favourite way to travel. I've rushed from place to place, attempting to fill every second with seeing all of the sites, and returned home exhausted. Instead now I much prefer to take it slowly and really experience the culture of where I am. My favourite trips have been ones spent in one place for a long time, really taking everything in and not pressuring myself to do anything but enjoy where I am.

Slow travel can be in the form of taking the train to get somewhere slowly and enjoying the beautiful landscape along the way. Or staying in one location for two weeks and getting to know all the immediate surroundings really well during your stay. Slow travel really lends itself to sustainable travel, as taking your time to get somewhere – by train rather than plane, or cycling or walking from place to place instead of driving – is far less damaging to the environment. Plus, if you're opting out of paying to see lots of different tourist sites, or staying in one place rather than paying for transport all over, you'll save yourself some money too!

So much of travel has become a way of ticking off a list: of things to see and countries we've visited. It is all such a rush making sure you've done all the things that everyone says you have to do, or seeing the thing everyone says you must see. Filling every day with a busy schedule that if you deviate from you won't have the time to 'fit everything in'. Now, travelling fast can sometimes be a good thing. Like everything in life, it's about balance. But it's important that if our lives are typically going at 100mph, travel is our opportunity to slow down, rather than continue this fast pace. What if you let go of the expectations or lists, and just go with the flow? Slow down and decide how *you* would like to enjoy your time? Give yourself more time to do fewer things, but do them *fully*. Get off our phones, relax into our surroundings and reconnect to the world.

## How to travel slowly

### DITCH THE PLANS

I love an itinerary, don't get me wrong. Planning ahead to understand where you're going and what you can do is a great way to get the most out of your holiday. However, sometimes it's just as much (if not more) fun to ditch the plans and just see how things go. I like to do this at least a few days out of my trip: just wander around, eat at places that I see along the way, walk down streets that intrigue me and see the sites that catch my eye. There are no expectations, no time frames, no buses to catch or reservations to make. Just a new place you've never been to enjoy and explore.

## LEARN THE LANGUAGE

Ahead of your trip, do a bit of research about the language and learn some key phrases to get you by. No one is expecting you to be able to speak the language of everywhere you go, and if you're lucky enough to have English as your first language, the road is a lot easier for you. But learning simple phrases such as 'hello', 'how are you', 'thank you', 'please', or 'good evening', can allow you to connect more to the locals and show them that you're trying.

## GET OFF THE PATH

Get adventurous and go off the path that other tourists follow. Seeing the main sites is a wonderful way to get to know a new place, but so is exploring without any guide or map. Browse with an open-minded curiosity about the area you're visiting, and don't be afraid to be adventurous in new ways.

## SPEAK TO THE LOCALS

If you're lucky enough to know a local wherever you're visiting, then make the most of it! Listen to their advice on what to do and see, and get to know the area like a local does. If you don't know anybody, then get to know them! Speak to the people at restaurants, cafes and shops. Ask them about their experience in their home, how long they've lived there, their favourite places, where they go in the evenings, what their favourite thing to do is. Don't be afraid to spark up conversation, make friends and understand how people in different places live. We get so soaked up in our own lives, our phones, our individual homes and circles of friends, that we forget to look outside of it and *speak* to people. I know because I do it! But I like to force myself to step outside of my comfort zone and build my confidence up to talk to the locals and hear their stories.

## DO AS THE LOCALS DO

In the same vein, take a local's advice and do as they do! See how they live, how they eat, and join in with what they do! It's too easy to slip into our own habits and routines, visit familiar places and shop at familiar shops. But look beyond this to find out new and different ways to do things that you may have never tried before.

Not only will this help you to understand a new place better, but it will leave you with amazing memories and enable you to connect to a place and its people in an unforgettable way.

STAY STILL

Travel in its nature implies movement, to go somewhere on a journey. But on this journey we have to remember to stop and just stay still. Take a moment to just soak it all in. Wake up in the morning and instead of immediately heading out to the first must-see tourist spot, take a moment to enjoy a slow breakfast, sip some morning coffee and watch the world go by. When visiting a site you want to see, pause and take it in rather than moving with the crowd. Spend time to understand the history and absorb its beauty.

There is definitely a time and place for 'fast travel' if your trip is short or you know you'll never be back. Maybe you're just in the mood to see everything there is to see! Nevertheless, slow travel is something we can all think about incorporating to really absorb where we are, live in the moment and let go of any pressure. We are so used to moving fast in all other areas of our lives, that when on holiday or on a trip it can be easy to continue this pace. Instead, give slowing it down a go, and see how it feels.

# eight

—

# self-care

# What is Self-care?

With the rise in movements such as body positivity and increasing awareness around mental health, more and more people are talking about self-care and self-love. And I'm all for it.

It's human nature to find faults with ourselves. We live in our own bodies and minds every single day. We pick apart our bad bits and feel like a failure when we don't achieve what we want. This is why loving ourselves and setting aside time to take care of ourselves is so important. When minimising and aiming to be more sustainable, we mustn't discard our own needs and happiness.

The hustle and bustle of modern living and pressure to succeed makes self-care more important than ever before. I'm not convinced the way we live our lives is what humans are designed to do; the constant pressure to earn money and be successful, longer working weeks and less leisure time leave many people feeling empty. And it's no surprise to me that this way of life is in turn damaging to the environment (more work = more money = more consumption = more carbon emissions and waste). I want to see more of us able to prioritise our own self-care, no matter what commitments we have in life, and regardless of the situations we are in. It's more than just a buzzword or trendy phrase right now, it's crucial to maintaining happiness in a busy, fast-paced and demanding world.

Practising self-care is a journey rather than a destination. In this chapter I will share all of my best advice, but trust me when I say I also struggle to implement these habits – particularly when life gets hard. It isn't easy juggling the demands of each day and the behaviours that we know are good for us. It's during times when your life is chaotic that taking care of yourself is the *most* important. It's also during these times that it can be the most difficult. But there is a silver lining! If we make these actions habits, then they can see us through difficult times. It's these simple acts that we have to put first in order to keep ourselves going.

Self-love is about appreciating and taking care of yourself, and knowing what's best for you. Neglecting basic things – such as giving yourself a break, eating well, getting enough sleep, moving your body or talking to people about your problems – can quickly lead to a downward spiral for our mental and physical health. Let's stop this from happening, and learn how to put *you* first.

## Minimising your life

Minimalism is about minimising your *life*, not just the physical things in it. It's about what you do, who you spend your time with, what media and information you consume, your mindset and your experiences. As you physically declutter you'll start to notice the effect it will have on your mental wellbeing. How clearing your home gives you more mental clarity. How getting rid of stuff allows the space and opportunity to focus on what's important. How freeing up your schedule can allow time for more meaningful pursuits.

There are so many things that I decluttered from my life that weren't in my wardrobe or my kitchen. And in many ways this is a bigger task. I used to binge drink every week to bury my problems. I had to face up to the fact that this was a problem and I needed to stop, so I quit drinking. I used to be far too obsessed and preoccupied with my appearance, so I stopped wearing so much makeup, quit diet culture and gave up caring about fashion. I was unhappy in my job and fed up with how I was being treated, so I decided to quit and pursue something new. These were all very hard decisions that took so much courage. There were a lot of tears, many embarrassing phone calls to my family, and even more second guessing. I had to face my problems front on, look deeply at myself and who I was, and change the things that weren't right. And you can do this too.

Answer the following questions to begin to understand what might be stopping you in your life from getting where you want to be, or causing you unhappiness and stress:

- What am I doing each day that I don't want to be doing?
- What do I want to be doing instead?
- What unhealthy habits are keeping me from achieving what I want in life?
- What healthy habits could I replace these with?
- Is there anyone in my life that causes distraction, negativity and insecurities?
- Who in my life makes me feel good, that I can trust and supports me?
- Am I stressed? Why is this?
- What can I do to de-stress on a more regular basis?
- Is there one thing I can pinpoint that is making me unhappy?
- Is there one thing I can pinpoint that makes me happy?

Hopefully after thinking through these questions it has become a lot clearer what needs to change in your life. We could all do with looking over a list like this once in a while to consider what we're doing and why, and whether it's making us happy. If there is something big sticking out after going over these questions, now is the time to consider a plan of action to change things for the better. I know this can be seriously hard, but it is so important to face challenges in order to be happier. Short-term pain for long-term gain.

## Goal setting

So we can start making changes, let's set some goals! Setting goals is a great way to become clear about what you want to achieve, and staying on track to make that happen.

First, write down a list of your goals. Try separating them into sections, such as personal goals and career goals. Use the template opposite, but also go into more detail in your own notebook.

Start with a bigger and more comprehensive list of goals you want to achieve in life, from small ones, such as taking up yoga, to bigger goals such as landing your dream job. This can be a useful practice to take up at the start of each year.

At the beginning of each month write up specific goals and tasks that you think you can achieve that month. If you have noted that you want to start doing yoga, for example, in your monthly goals you can aim to do yoga once or twice a week to make this happen. Be even more specific by saying whether you'd follow a video at home, or go to a class. Which videos, and which class? At what time of day can you fit this in? Be specific, be realistic, but also try to push yourself. Setting these targets and actions will help you get to where you want to be.

At the end of each month, look over your goals and evaluate what you have or haven't achieved, why that's happened and how you can move forward next time. You may have been overambitious with some goals that you need to reconsider, or you may have been focussing on career goals at the expense of personal goals. Pat yourself on the back for what you have achieved, and never beat yourself up for what you haven't. Just think about why it might have been, and come up with a solution for you to get there next month. It's normal to miss the mark on some goals, and prioritise others. You'll get better at this process over time, understanding how long something takes you, and where you tend to prioritise or procrastinate.

|  | How will I achieve this? | When by? |
|---|---|---|
| PERSONAL GOALS | | |
| Short-term goal 1 | | |
| Short-term goal 2 | | |
| Long-term goal 1 | | |
| Long-term goal  2 | | |
| CAREER GOALS | | |
| Short-term goal 1 | | |
| Short-term goal 2 | | |
| Long-term goal 1 | | |
| Long-term goal 2 | | |

## Organising your time

After setting goals, making sure that you use your time wisely is key to achieving them. Not only that, but creating a better work/life balance means that you'll get your to-do list done, while also having time in your week for hobbies and chilling out. Freeing up space on your schedule can allow you to get where you want to be, while enjoying your life at the same time. What a novelty! Knowing your priorities and making sure you fit these into your day will transform how you feel and what you can achieve.

Looking over your goals at the start of each week can help to make them happen. If you like lists, then write a weekly to-do to reference each day. And like everything else, less is more. Don't spread yourself thin each day; set realistic goals and tasks that over time you can build on.

### WRITE IT DOWN SOMEWHERE

There are lots of different ways you can stay organised and set out tasks, meetings or events, such as a bullet journal, a yearly planner, or online platforms such as Trello. I often let things swim around in my head until I realise I've forgotten to do something or that something was coming up. This can lead to extra unnecessary stress. Writing it down will keep you calm and organise your time.

### DAILY TO-DO

Every work day, write down a short to-do list. Don't make the list too long, so that you stay realistic about what you can achieve in one day. If you don't get something done, then just move it onto the top of tomorrow's list.

### GET QUICK THINGS DONE FIRST

If something takes less than a couple of minutes to do, get it done first. That could be replying to a particular email, tidying something away, making a phone call or doing a boring bit of admin. This means you can get one thing ticked off before you've even really begun!

## DON'T PUT THINGS OFF

If there is something on your daily to-dos that keeps on getting pushed to the next day, then prioritise it at the start of the day to make sure it gets done. It can be easy to put the most important or enjoyable things first, and let more boring or difficult things slide, but get it out of the way so you can forget about it. Future you will thank you for it.

## SCHEDULE IN BREAKS

Being productive is as important as taking time off. During your day, week and month, schedule time off for yourself. Take a walk at lunchtime, have at least one day a week with no plans, or arrange to do something fun each month with friends and family. Allow yourself to relax, and enjoy the feeling of not doing anything. If you keep running at 100 miles per hour, you'll eventually burn out and won't be able to run at all. Making time for leisure and fun is what will keep you revitalised, passionate and excited about life and your goals.

## SAY NO

Our schedules can start filling up if we keep saying yes to everything. Knowing when to say no and learning how much time you realistically have will keep you afloat, rather than drowning in all of your commitments. Gain the courage to say no to things you don't want to do, or you don't have the time for.

## PRIORITISE

One of the best ways to organise your time is to learn to prioritise. Know what tasks are the most important, and don't procrastinate on things that need your attention. Doing things in order of priority will help you to get everything done. As you get into the habit of writing down your to-dos and goals, you will find it easier to see what things need to be a top priority in order to achieve what you want.

## Mindful daily tasks

Try to do as many things on this list as possible each day. Make it a habit and it'll become second nature!

1 TAKE A BREAK

Don't just work through the day without stopping. You're likely to find your mind wandering and your brain getting tired. Take regular breaks throughout the day to refresh.

2 STRETCH

During these breaks, stretch! If you're sitting at a desk all day, your body will appreciate the movement. Even if it's as simple as walking around the room and stretching your arms in the air, move those muscles to keep them alive.

3 EAT WITHOUT DISTRACTION

Instead of scoffing down your meal looking at your phone or watching the TV, try to mindfully eat at least once a day. Slow down, and just enjoy the food you're eating without distractions.

4 DO NOTHING

We're always setting ourselves tasks and things to do, but sometimes we should allow ourselves to just *be*. At one point in your day, do nothing at all. Sit and look out of the window, lie down and close your eyes, potter about the garden, without any task or intention in your head.

5 SWITCH OFF YOUR PHONE FOR ONE HOUR

We could all do with less time on our phones. Next time you need to complete a task, switch off your phone for an hour to help you finish it. Go that one step further and think about a digital detox.

6 DO ONE TASK AT A TIME

Try to complete one task at a time throughout your day rather than flicking between them. Set yourself an amount of time to spend on each one. This can help to get everything done, without distraction. One thing at a time.

7  BODY SCAN

This was one of the first ways I was introduced to a form
of meditation and mindfulness when I was a kid. It involves
scanning your body really slowly to check in with yourself.
Start in a comfortable position (lying down if you can), bring
awareness to your breath and close your eyes. Starting at the tip
of your head, slowly scan your body, paying attention to each
part. Your head, then your forehead, your ears and temples, your
eyes and cheeks, your nose and mouth, your chin and jaw. Make
your way down your whole body as slowly as possible, checking
in with each part until you reach the tips of your toes. Slowly
re-open your eyes and enjoy how relaxed you feel!

8  LOOK AT SOMETHING NATURAL

Whether you're outside in a park, on a beach, walking down
the street, or even sitting in the office, find something natural (if
inside, an indoor plant or piece of fruit, for example), and just
take it in. Think of the colours, shapes and textures (and even
sounds if you're outside). Let your thoughts pass by and just
focus on this piece of nature for a minute or two.

9  LISTEN

Instead of talking, or thinking, just listen. Listen to a friend, to
the noises outside, to relaxing music, to people talking around
you. Take yourself out of your own head and body and just
observe the sounds around you.

10 MAKE A GRATITUDE LIST

Every morning, write down three things that you are grateful
for. It can be anything from being grateful for a glass of water, to
grateful for your family. This practice will help you to focus on
what you are lucky to have in life, over what you *don't*.

### Morning routine

A mindful morning routine is a privilege you should reward yourself with every day. You wake up every morning with a fresh start, an opportunity to take care of yourself and have a productive day. I've got myself into so many ruts because I wasn't taking the time for myself in the mornings. I ended up feeling rushed, tired and in a bad mood before the day had even begun.

And that's where a morning routine comes in – figuring out what habits will set you up for the day on a positive note, that will get you out of bed on harder days, and will make you focus on living in the moment. I wrote a list of the key things I wanted to be doing each morning to help get me back on track:

1   Get up early (6–7am)
2   Go outside
3   Exercise
4   Slow breakfast
5   Moment of gratitude

Your list might include completely different things; just set goals that make you feel happy. And on the days that are harder to get out of bed, achieving even just one of the things on your list should be celebrated. Even when you feel fed up or down, the power of a routine is amazing at setting ourselves into motions that we know make us feel good.

## Your key morning habits:

..............................................  ..............................................

..............................................  ..............................................

..............................................  ..............................................

..............................................  ..............................................

# My Self-care Tips

Now that we've set goals, organised our time and learnt how to be more mindful throughout our day, let's get stuck into some self-care. Taking care of yourself can be in any form that makes you feel healthy, happy and thriving. Below are my favourite ways to show myself a little love, that I think will make you feel pretty great too!

1 SLEEPING

I don't know about you, but as soon as I don't get enough sleep, I start to become moody, unproductive and anxious. I just can't function properly! It's so easy to neglect sleep – we can manage with a couple of hours less, right? While occasionally not getting a good night's sleep won't do any harm, consistently not sleeping well will have an accumulative effect on your wellbeing. Make sure to get enough shuteye, especially during times when you're particularly busy or overwhelmed. After all, this is when you'll need it the most! Go to bed an hour earlier (put that phone away), take a quick nap, establish a relaxing night-time routine, or let yourself sleep in for an extra hour in the morning to recharge. Listen to your body and make sure you don't get too run down from lack of sleep.

2 PAMPERING

I really stop caring about how I look, brushing my hair, putting on makeup, or wearing anything other than leggings and an oversized jumper when I'm not feeling my best. So a way to inject some self-love is to pamper yourself a little! Take time out of your day to have a long bath, put on a face mask, wear some sparkly eyeshadow or an outfit that always makes you feel your best. It's surprising how neglecting our hygiene and appearance can really affect how we feel mentally, and vice versa. Showing yourself some love by taking care of your body is the perfect way to bring back some of your confidence.

3   GOING OUTSIDE

There's something about nature that brings you back down to earth. The small or big things that are worrying you seem to shrink when you take a step outside into nature and absorb the sights, smells and sounds around you. Even if you live in a city, find some green space near you and take a walk, breathe it in and switch off. Take the time to remember how beautiful this Earth is, how lucky you are to be alive, and that while your head may feel scrambled, the Earth around you remains calm.

4   GETTING MOVING

Physical activity and exercise is my sanctuary. It gives one time in my day to totally switch off and focus on the strength of my body. I've never regretted going to the gym and getting a sweat on as I always leave feeling better!

The focus for the benefits of exercise is typically on our physical health, but what about our mental health? Exercise releases endorphins, releases tension and acts as meditation and a break from the everyday. Feeling strong, getting sweaty and exerting some energy is just what the doctor ordered when you're feeling a bit off. Find a sport, exercise or activity that you love and that you can realistically implement into your day-to-day life. A half an hour walk in nature, a 20-minute at-home HIIT workout, badminton with your friends or a swim in the sea – it doesn't matter what exercise you do, just do it! Stay consistent and make it a habit to take care of your physical and mental health as a unit that helps each other along.

5   BREATHING

Breathing is a very powerful tool that can be used at any time of any day to temper your mood and calm you down. Wherever you are, if you're beginning to feel that tightness in your chest, try concentrating on your breathing. Start by closing or lowering your eyes, and listen to the sound of your breath. Is it fast? Is it short? Listen, but don't judge, and acknowledge the sound of your own breath. From there, slow down your breathing, focusing on the rise and fall of your body. Imagine it like a wave from your stomach up to your chest. Slow down

the breathing, lengthening each breath in and each breath out.
Let any thoughts that pop into your head pass by, guiding your
attention back to your breath. Repeat this for at least a minute,
bringing your breath back to normal. When you're ready, slowly
open your eyes. Hopefully this practice will leave you feeling
more calm and relaxed than before you began. Sometimes
we need a minute or so to stop rushing and working, to
just breathe.

6   PUTTING DOWN YOUR PHONE

We're totally addicted to our phones. To social media. To
knowing what's happening on the other side of the world.
To our work. To checking in with friends online. The world
within our phones can be very distracting from the real world.
I find myself habitually picking up my phone without any
intention, getting sucked in to checking my social media, and
I'm not even sure why. Boredom? FOMO? Distraction? We
underestimate how much this habit affects how we feel as we
compare our lives to a stranger's and hear about news we didn't
need to hear.

7   GETTING COSY

Getting comfy and cosy is sometimes all you need to make you
feel better. Look after yourself like you would a child, and wrap
yourself up in a snuggly jumper, put on some cosy socks, light
some candles, make yourself a cup of tea and unwind with a
happy movie or soppy book. Even *thinking* about it makes me
feel calm.

8   STARTING A HOBBY

It's hard to find time for hobbies nowadays with our busy
schedules. We're so focused on the hustle and being 'productive',
we forget to have fun and do things outside of our comfort
zone. And as a result we're missing out on so many fun,
enriching and exciting pastimes! Think back to your childhood
and all the things you would do for no other reason than
because they were fun. Why aren't we doing more of this as
adults? Our adulting responsibilities shouldn't be allowed to take

over our lust for life. Take up a hobby that has no connection
to work or your life goals, such as playing the piano, painting,
playing tennis, surfing, reading, volunteering, dancing, writing –
anything that makes you happy!

9 TAKING TIME OFF

Life isn't always about going going going. It's in the downtime
that you can reflect, repair and rejuvenate. If you haven't taken
time off recently, then now is the time. You deserve a break!
Plan a day at the weekend with no plans whatsoever (shocking,
I know). Go away for the weekend, even if it isn't far. Ask if
friends and family can help out for a day or an evening if you
have kids or pets, and give yourself the time off that you deserve.

10 TALKING ABOUT IT

Finally, you must must must talk to people if you're feeling off.
So many of us go about life pretending to be fine, keep ticking
along until it all gets too much and everything snaps. Stop that
from happening, and open up to someone close to you. Don't
allow bad thoughts to sit in your head to develop a voice of
their own. Talking about your feelings is one of the best ways to
overcome and process these irrational thoughts. You don't need
an answer, or solutions; sometimes all you need is to just let it all
out. Pay yourself the biggest act of self-care by reaching out and
opening up.

11 NEVER COMPARING

As a bonus eleventh tip I want to touch on comparison.

Comparison is never a good thing, as the only person we
should ever compare ourself to is ourselves. And now, we have a
much bigger pool of people to compare ourselves to with social
media at our fingertips. People used to look up to celebrities
and compare the shape of their body to theirs, or feel jealous
of their money and fame. Now, we have ordinary people from
all over the world to compare ourselves to *as well*. There is
always someone more attractive, more successful, more wealthy,
more happy and more travelled. But these people may not
have your unique talents, relationships or individual successes.

Comparing ourselves and wanting what someone else has will get us nowhere. Remember to differentiate between inspiration and comparison, and don't allow yourself to think that what someone else has is better than what you have.

## Living in the present

This is probably the biggest thing that I struggle with day to day. I'm naturally very anxious and always have been; I constantly worry about what I've said or done in the past, or things that could happen in the future. My mind is always thinking of everything all at once and I find it particularly difficult to focus on what's happening right now without getting distracted by what's to come.

I have, however, learnt ways to tackle this. It doesn't come naturally, so I have to work that little bit harder to stop worrying and start living. Here are some things that really help to live in the present.

### LETTING GO

Having grudges, analysing conversations or going over situations that have been and gone is a surefire way to waste unnecessary energy on the past. Learning how to let go can be really difficult at times, particularly if something has been traumatic. But allowing yourself to leave it behind and move forward is one of the most powerful decisions you can make for yourself. Someone once told me that holding a grudge is like allowing someone to live inside your head without paying rent. Holding on to that pain and anger won't get you anywhere. Over-analysing situations will only make you paranoid and miserable. There is no use in going over the silly thing you said, the way a bad situation panned out or how someone else acted. Learn from it if necessary, and move on. It's hard, but with practice and strength, you can do it.

### DOING THINGS WITH NO OUTCOME

How many things do you do each day that have no outcome?
No goal, target or result? Everything we do is in order to achieve
something in return. Going to work to get paid. Studying to pass a
test. Dressing up to impress. Waking up early to be more productive.
What if we just did things without any outcome in mind? We fill
our days with productivity, entertainment and activities to reach our
goals. And no wonder we feel stressed out: we aren't giving ourselves
a break! When was the last time you did something for no particular
purpose? Do something today just because you want to, not because
you believe it will get you closer to a particular goal.

### BEING MINDFUL OF WHAT YOU ABSORB

Every day we are surrounded by lots of different information.
From adverts on the Tube, to posts on social media, to reports on
the news. It's likely that the information that you are absorbing
each day is having an effect on how you feel. If we are constantly
absorbing outside information that doesn't aid us, we can easily
become distracted, disheartened and anxious. As I've mentioned
before, be careful of who you follow on social media, but also be
aware of what information and media you are absorbing elsewhere.
Is a TV show you've been recommended stressing you out, despite
it being highly reviewed? Does listening to the news upset you
more than it informs you? Are a friend's comments triggering
your eating disorder? Take yourself away from outside information
that doesn't sit well with you, and be wary of what information
you consume.

# Taking Care of Your Body and Mind

The connection between our body and mind is closer than we think. Our gut and brain, for example, are constantly sending messages to one another, affecting how the other acts. If nerves have ever caused butterflies in your stomach, or a bout of anxiety has made you feel sick, you'll know this only too well. We all know that moving our bodies releases endorphins that makes us feel good, but getting out of the habit of exercise can make it even trickier to start. Worrying about something can lead to not sleeping, and not sleeping can cause even more worrying. Losing a routine can make taking care of our physical and mental health hard, but there are ways to regain this routine and always make self-care a priority.

I find that if I am not taking care of the basic necessities of sleep, water, food, exercise and relaxation, it begins to take its toll on my mental health. If I am hungry, I can barely form a sentence, and if I get out of the routine of exercising, I stop feeling like myself. Anxious feelings and negative thought patterns will creep up a lot easier if you don't take care of your fundamental human needs.

Of course, mental health goes far beyond what we're eating or how much sleep we're getting, but the questions over the page can be a good indicator of whether we are giving ourselves the care we deserve. If you're struggling with your mental health, please get in touch with your doctor or a healthcare professional to make sure you're receiving the support and medical assistance needed. If you broke your arm, you wouldn't avoid going to the hospital, so if your brain isn't feeling happy and you're finding it difficult to take care of the items mentioned here, please reach out for help.

So if you're feeling off, ask yourself one of the questions below, and find out if there could be an immediate solution to the problem. It often helps to put a reason behind why you are feeling how you are, that is outside of yourself.

- Are you getting enough sleep? Are you struggling to fall asleep?
- Are you drinking enough water?
- Do you have a balanced relationship with food? Are you eating enough? Are you eating what makes you feel good?
- Are you taking the time out of each day to move your body in a way that makes you feel good? Do you have a healthy relationship with exercise?
- Are you resting and giving yourself time to relax and unwind? Do you feel overworked?

## Sleep

If you're struggling to sleep, or staying up too late, try to establish a routine. Switch technology off at least an hour before bed and set up a relaxing evening routine such as taking a bath or reading a book before bed. Going to bed earlier can help develop a routine and give you time to unwind before bed.

## Water

Make sure to stay hydrated throughout your day to keep alert and feeling your best. A great way to make sure you're drinking enough is to always have a bottle with you filled with water to sip on throughout your day. Keep an eye on the colour of your urine throughout the day, aiming to keep it a lighter rather than dark yellow colour.

## Food

Food is a sensitive topic, and something so many of us find tricky to balance. Make sure you're eating enough, not neglecting your body but listening to its needs. Diet culture has us believing we should ignore our hunger cues and restrict ourselves, but try to get away from this mentality if it's negatively affecting you, and head towards a more intuitive approach to eating. A diet filled with vegetables *and* chocolate is my idea of balance. Variety, balance and no restriction. Disordered eating habits shouldn't be ignored, whether that's undereating, restricting certain food groups, or binge eating. So be aware of your relationship with food, get help if you need it, and remove labels such as 'good' and 'bad' from the foods you're eating.

## Movement

Find a form of movement that you enjoy, and keep doing it! Anything counts, from walking, to running, weightlifting or tennis. It doesn't matter how you get up and moving, just that it's something that is sustainable for your lifestyle. Make it fun, and focus on doing it to take care of your physical and mental health. If you're out of the habit of exercising, set a time during your day that you will move your body, and soon it will become a part of your daily routine.

## Rest

Potentially one of the most important things of all is rest. Don't neglect a good bit of R&R. You won't be very good at exercising, eating well, drinking enough water or even sleeping if you aren't giving yourself time off. Your work will benefit, your relationships will benefit and your health will benefit. Set aside at least one hour a day for rest, to go for a walk, read a book, chill out on the sofa or do something else that relaxes you. Similarly, put time aside at the weekends and each month to rest.

# Mental and Physical Health Comes First

I want to finish this chapter, and this book, discussing how our health always comes first. It's no good trying to save the planet, reduce your waste and minimise your life if you aren't happy or healthy. If any of these tasks become taxing, then *stop*. Veganism isn't for everyone, neither is going plastic-free. And small misgivings such as using a plastic cup or buying fast fashion aren't going to ruin the world alone. It doesn't make you a bad person, it just makes your situation different. Making minimalism and sustainability accessible to *all* means valuing the individual mental health, physical health, economic background and culture of each person. Acknowledge if you're finding it tough, or if you're being too hard on yourself, and find the right balance for you.

We can't expect to change the world if we are suffering ourselves. How will you be capable of meal prepping, remembering to bring your own reusables or learning about climate change, if you're suffering with your health? I can answer for you. You won't. Always put *you* first. *You* are a part of this world, and *you* deserve to feel happy and healthy. If we take care of ourselves, we can take care of the Earth we share.

# Epilogue

Oh hey there sustainable minimalist! You made it through the book, and I can only hope that some things have changed since the day you first opened it. Stop and think about the changes you've made (even if those changes are being made inside your head for now). And give yourself a pat on the back! It's easy to forget all the good things we've done, so take this moment to notice how much has changed and how far you've come.

Refer back to this book as you learn to implement many of these new habits into your routine. As this is such a comprehensive guide, it's going to take time to digest and make many of these switches. I know I'll even be dipping back in myself for some motivational reminders! Allow yourself time, and have patience to make the changes truly sustainable in your life.

Remember, if all of your family and friends think you're a bit mad, talk to them! Give them this book! Explain to them why it's important what you're doing, and why they should be giving it a go too. The more we engage with one another and have an open discussion about the way we live our lives and how we need to adapt accordingly, the more likely we are to tackle the problem head on. There is no use in sitting on an island alone, making all the effort as nobody around us joins in. Lead by example, have discussions (try to avoid arguments!), and teach what you have learnt. Make your family and friends an amazing vegan meal, give them a reusable bag to take to the shops or watch a documentary with them about climate change. It can be frustrating if these efforts are met with apathy, but try your best and keep doing what you're doing. You'd be surprised the impact you can have over time on those around you.

Throughout this book I have emphasised how much you should never guilt yourself into doing anything in the name of 'sustainability' or 'minimalism'. We all need to know our boundaries and limits when it comes to making big lifestyle changes. However, I also want you to be honest about what you *can* do and go at it with your best effort. If you're in a position where you have access to vegan food and can swap out animal products easily, such as switching cow's milk for plant milk, then go for it! Similarly if you're buying a lot of fast fashion, think about the difference you could make if you quit this habit and slowed down your intake. If you've always voted for the same political party, or been on the same energy supplier for years, then change it for the greener option! Once you have the information I've given you and know about the impacts of your daily actions, it's your responsibility to avoid those that are harmful, that you are *able* to. We need more and more people to step outside of their comfort zone and make the changes that are needed. What's stopping you?

Continue to research, keep learning and understand the politics behind climate change. Find out why it's happening, what must be done and why it's so important we respond now. It's more than just making individual lifestyle swaps, but making big societal changes. Both of which you can play a huge part in. Let's do it!

# Acknowledgements

First I want to thank my publishers Ebury Press at Penguin Random House and my publisher Michelle Warner, who came to me with the wonderful opportunity to write this book. I will always be shocked, and so thankful, that you chose me for this amazing project. Thanks to Paul Simpson, my copy-editor, for fixing all of my mistakes and perfecting the text; Chloe Rose and Katie Sadler for getting this book out to the world; Anya Kurvarzina for illustrating it so beautifully; and Emily Voller for her gorgeous design. Thank you to the whole team at Ebury Press for working so hard on this book and believing in me.

Next is a big thank you to my partner in crime, Alex, without whom I wouldn't have been able to finish this book in time. You got me back on a straight path every time I fell off. Thank you to my number one fan from the beginning, my mum. Thank you to my dad Mick, my sister Charlie and my soon-to-be brother-in-law Tom for all being there during the highs and lows.

Thank you to Ali for always listening and brainstorming ideas. Thank you Immy, my best online turned real-life friend. Thank you to the too many to mention online who have inspired and educated me, and are paving the way for a better world. A huge thank you to my management MC Saatchi Social and my amazing manager, Paige Jones, who has supported, advised and guided me throughout this project. You saw something in me and I'm glad that I've been able to repay your faith with this book.

And last but certainly not least, a massive thank you to my audience and readers. Without your support, I wouldn't have been given this opportunity.

# Resources

For more information on all the topics discussed in this book find me online:

Madeleine Olivia

www.madeleineolivia.co.uk    @MadeleineOlivia

## DOCUMENTARIES

Before the Flood
www.beforetheflood.com

Chasing Coral
www.chasingcoral.com
@chasingcoral

Cowspiracy
www.cowspiracy.com
@cowspiracy

Earthlings
www.nationearth.com
@EarthlingsMovie

An Inconvenient Truth
www.algore.com
@algore

Minimalism: A Documentary
www.theminimalists.com
@TheMinimalists

The Need to Grow
grow.foodrevolution.org
@TheNeedToGrow

Our Planet
www.ourplanet.com
@ourplanet

A Plastic Ocean
www.aplasticocean.movie

The True Cost
www.truecostmovie.com
@truecostmovie

## BOOKS

Michael Braungart and William McDonough, *Cradle to Cradle: Remaking the Way We Make Things* (Vintage, 2009)

Martin Dorey, *No. More. Plastic* (Ebury Press, 2018)

Kathryn Kellogg, *101 Ways to Go Zero Waste* (Countryman Press, 2019)

Naomi Klein, *This Changes Everything: Capitalism vs the Climate* (Penguin Books, 2015)

Elizabeth Kolbert, *Field Notes from a Catastrophe: Man, Nature and Climate Change* (Bloomsbury, 2015)

Mary Kondo, *The Life-Changing Magic of Tidying Up: The Japanese Art of Decluttering and Organizing* (Vermilion, 2014)

Grey McKeown, *Essentialism: The Disciplined Pursuit of Less* (Virgin Books, 2014)

Michael Pollan, *In Defense of Food: An Eater's Manifesto* (Penguin Books, 2009)

Jonathan Safran Foer, *Eating Animals* (Penguin Books, 2011)

Lucy Siegle, *To Die For: Is Fashion Wearing Out the World?* (Fourth Estate, 2011)

Sean Spicer, *Overdressed: The Shockingly High Cost of Cheap Fashion* (Portfolio, 2013)

## ORGANISATIONS

Ecocide Law
www.stopecocide.earth
@EcocideLaw

Ethical Consumer
www.ethicalconsumer.org
@EC_magazine

Extinction Rebellion
www.rebellion.earth/
@ExtinctionR

Fashion Revolution
www.fashionrevolution.org
@fash_rev

Greenpeace
www.greenpeace.org.uk
@Greenpeace

WWF
www.wwf.org.uk
@wwf_uk

## WEBSITES

Bosh
www.bosh.tv
@BOSHTV

Cruelty Free Kitty
www.crueltyfreekitty.com
@crueltyfreecat

Flight Free
www.flightfree.co.uk
@FlightFree2020

Good On You
www.goodonyou.eco
@GoodOnyou_App

Green Matters
www.greenmatters.com
@GreenMatters

Low Impact Movement
www.lowimpactmovement.org

Logical Harmony
www.logicalharmony.net
@logicalharmony

So Vegan
www.wearesovegan.com
@wearesovegan

Vegan Beauty Girl
www.veganbeautygirl.co.uk
@veganbeautygirl

Vegan Richa
www.veganricha.com
@veganricha

Zero Waste Chef
www.zerowastechef.com
@ZeroWasteChef

# Endnotes

1   Joshua Fields Millburn & Ryan Nicodemus, www.theminimalists.com/minimalism/

2   Matt McGrath, 'Climate change: 12 years to save the planet? Make that 18 months', www.bbc.co.uk/news/, 24 July 2019

3   Eurostat, 'Waste Statistics' ec.europa.eu/eurostat, June 2019

4   Gov.uk, 'UK statistics on waste', www.gov.uk, 7 March 2019

5   Daniel Hoornweg and Perinaz Bhada-Tata, 'What A Waste: A Global Review of Solid Waste Management', siteresources.worldbank.org, March 2012

6   Zoë Lenkiewicz, 'Marine Plastic Pollution: From the Land to the Sea', wasteaid.org, 25 August 2018

7   Ellen MacArthur Foundation, 'The new plastics economy: Rethinking the future of plastics & Catalysing action', www.ellenmacarthurfoundation.org, 13 December 2017

8   Martin Dorey, *No. More. Plastic* (Ebury Press, 2018) p.57

9   United Nations, 'SAVE FOOD: Global Initiative on Food Loss and Waste Reduction', www.fao.org/save-food/resources, 2019

10  Rebecca Smithers, 'UK throwing away £13bn of food each year, latest figures show', www.theguardian.com, 10 January 2017

11  Pasty Perry, 'The environment costs of fast fashion', www.independent.co.uk, 8 January 2018

12  Roger Harrabin, 'Fast fashion is harming the planet, MPs say', www.bbc.co.uk/news, 5 October 2018

13  ibid

14  Nadia Khomami, 'Burberry destroys £28m of stock to guard against counterfeits', www.theguardian.com, 19 July 2018

15  Roger Harrabin, 'Fast fashion is harming the planet, MPs say', www.bbc.co.uk/news, 5 October 2018

16  Tansy Hoskins, 'Is the fur trade sustainable?', www.theguardian.com, 29 October 2013

17  U.S. Environmental Protection Agency, 'Regis Tannery', *Waste Site Cleanup and Reuse in New England*, 9 August 2006

18  S.K. Rastogi et al. (2007), 'Occupational Cancers in Leather Tanning Industries: A Short Review', *Indian Journal of Occupational and Environmental Medicine* 11

19  Mimi Bekhechi, 'A wool jumper is just as cruel as a mink coat', www.independent.co.uk, 16 July 2014

20  Animals Australia, 'Mulesing', www.animalsaustralia.org, 2014

21  Lyst, 'Searching for sustainability', www.lyst.com, 2019

22 Statista, 'Market value of beauty and personal care in the United Kingdom (UK) from 2015 to 2020 (in million euros)', www.statista.com, 5 June 2019 (paywall)

23 Jessica Morgan, 'Is the beauty industry doing enough to tackle plastic pollution?', www.independent.co.uk, 31 January 2019

24 Roddy Scheer and Doug Moss, 'Should People Be Concerned about Parabens in Beauty Products?', www.scientificamerican.com, 6 October 2014

25 US National Library of Medicine National Institutes of Health, 'Formaldehyde-releasers in cosmetics in the USA and in Europe', www.ncbi.nlm.nih.gov/, 3 March 2010

26 Sonali K. Doke and Shashikant C. Dhawale, 'Alternatives to animal testing: A review', reprinted at US National Library of Medicine National Institutes of Health, www.ncbi.nlm.nih.gov, 18 November 2013
Humane Society International, 'Costs of Animal and Non-Animal Testing', www.hsi.org, 23 October 2012

27 DivaCup, 'Eco-Divas', divacup.com, 2017

28 Lindsay Wilson, 'The carbon foodprint of 5 diets compared', shrinkthatfootprint.com, 2012

29 EarthDay, 'Climate Change–Cutting Your Foodprint', www.earthday.org, 2019

30 Marco Springmann, 'Plant-based diets could save millions of lives and dramatically cut greenhouse gas emissions', www.oxfordmartin.ox.ac.uk, 21 March 2016

31 Damian Carrington, 'Avoiding meat and dairy is "single biggest way" to reduce your impact on Earth', www.theguardian.com, 31 May 2018

32 United Nations, 'Livestock's Long Shadow', www.fao.org, 2006

33 Yale School of Forestry & Environmental Studies, 'Cattle Ranching in the Amazon Region', globalforestatlas.yale.edu, 2015

34 *Cowspiracy: The Sustainability Secret* (dir. Kip Andersen and Keegan Kuhn, 2014)

35 John Roach, 'Seafood May Be Gone by 2048, Study Says', www.nationalgeographic.com, 2 November 2006

36 Scarborough, P., Appleby, P.N., Mizdrak, A. et al. *Climatic Change* (2014) 125: 179. www.doi.org/10.1007/s10584-014-1169-1

37 Kari Hamerschlag, 'Climate and Environmental Impacts', www.ewg.org, 2011

38 Gidon Eshela, 1,2, Alon Sheponb, 1, Tamar Makovc, and Ron Milo, 'Land, irrigation water, greenhouse gas, and reactive nitrogen burdens of meat, eggs, and dairy production in the United States', www.pnas.org, 23 June 2014

39 Poore, J. & Nemecek, T. (2018). 'Reducing food's environmental impacts through producers and consumers', *Science* 360 pp. 987–992

40 EarthDay, 'Climate Change–Cutting Your Foodprint', www.earthday.org, 2019

41 Kari Hamerschlag, 'What You Eat Matters', www.ewg.org, 2011

42 Elisabeth Rosenthal, 'Once a Dream Fuel, Palm Oil May Be an Eco-Nightmare', www.nytimes.com, 31 January 2007

[43] Sam Wong, 'UK's carbon footprint from imported food revealed for first time', www.newscientist.com, 6 January 2016

[44] Food Ethics Council, 'Climate Change,' www.foodethicscouncil.org, 2019

[45] The Vegan Society, 'Compassion for Animals', www.vegansociety.com, 2019

[46] Andrew Wasley, Fiona Harvey, Madlen Davies and David Child, 'UK has nearly 800 livestock mega farms, investigation reveals', www.theguardian.com, 17 July 2017

[47] Marc Berkoff, 'Cows: Science Shows They're Bright and Emotional Individuals', www.psychologytoday.com, 2 November 2017

[48] David Jackson and Gary Marx, "Pork Producers Defend Gestation Crates, But Consumers Demand Change" *The Chicago Tribune*, 23 August 2016.

[49] Ferris Jabr, 'It's Official: Fish Feel Pain', www.smithsonianmag.com, 8 January 2018

[50] Peter Singer, 'Fish: the forgotten victims on our plate', www.theguardian.com, 14 September 2010

[51] Madeleine Howell and Gareth May, 'The hidden cruelty of the cashew industry – and the other fashionable foods that aren't as virtuous as they appear', www.telegraph.co.uk, 4 April 2019

[52] ibid

[53] Joshua Cooper, 'Our Oceans. Our Future. The United Nations Discusses Oceans', www.culturalsurvival.org, December 2017

[54] United Nations Permanent Forum on Indigenous Issues, 'Climate change and indigenous peoples', www.un.org, 2008

[55] Food Ethics Council, 'Food Waste,' www.foodethicscouncil.org, 2019

[56] *Hunger News*, '2018 World Hunger and Poverty Facts and Statistics', www.worldhunger.org, 25 April 2018

[57] The Vegan Society, www.vegansociety.com/go-vegan/definition-veganism

[58] *Vegan Easy,* 'Food Additives', www.veganeasy.org, 2019

[59] Christopher L. Weber and H. Scott Matthews, 'Food-Miles and the Relative Climate Impacts of Food Choices in the United States', pubs.acs.org, 16 April 2008

[60] BBC News, 'Is there a serious problem with coffee capsules?', www.bbc.co.uk, 19 February 2016

[61] Umair Irfan, 'Air travel is a huge contributor to climate change. A new global movement wants you to be ashamed to fly', www.vox.com, 1 August 2019

[62] Manfred Lenzen, Ya-Yen Sun, Futu Faturay, Yuan-Peng Ting, Arne Geschke & Arunima Malik, 'The carbon footprint of global tourism', www.nature.com, 7 May 2018

[63] Mark Smith, 'Cut your CO2 emissions by taking the train, by up to 90%...', www.seat61.com, 2019

[64] Dorey, *No. More. Plastic*, p125

# Index

Page references in italics indicate images